THE
MUSES' DARLING

Books by Charles Norman:

Poetry

THE BRIGHT WORLD

THE SAVAGE CENTURY

A SOLDIER'S DIARY

Biography

THE MUSES' DARLING

Cristofer Marlo

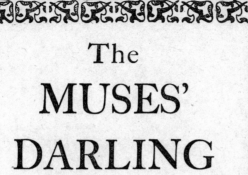

The
MUSES'
DARLING

The Life of
Christopher Marlowe

by

CHARLES NORMAN

Who euer lov'd, that lov'd not at first sight?

Rinehart & Company, Inc.

New York   Toronto

To

William McCleery

Contents

Illustrations

Collotypes printed by Paul L. Baruch

Foreword

I N that distant Elizabethan world thronged by shadowy
figures bearing great names, Christopher Marlowe is
the radiant one, 'the Muses' darling' in a contemporary's
praise.

His work and his personality have stirred the imaginations of many men. Charles Lamb wrote: 'The death-
scene of Marlowe's king moves pity and terror beyond
any scene, ancient or modern, with which I am acquainted.' To Lowell in America it was: 'With him I
grew acquainted during the impressible and receptive period of my youth. He was the first man of genius I had
ever really known, and he naturally bewitched me.' To
Shakespeare he was the only poet of his time worthy to be
quoted.

To read him today is to know again the youth of man
and the youth of the theater. The mere mention of his
name can excite even those who know him only by a few
lines learned in school. His fascination is the more extraordinary because we do not possess a single portrait or
description of him. We may assume that he went bearded
in the fashion of his age—that is all; but whether he wore
a trim, scholarly brush like Shakespeare; a fat, rounded
one like Jonson, a Jovian one like Chapman, or a long

and pointed one like Greene—whether he was tall or
short, or had blue eyes or brown or gray—we probably
shall never know. He is elusive. From school to early
death his name underwent remarkable variations: Marley
(the way he and his father wrote it) in Canterbury;
Marlin, Merling and Morley at Cambridge; Marle, Marlowe and other variations in London. Sometimes, as a result, he is almost lost to us in the welter of Elizabethan
documents; but we always know our man because his
troubles were consistent.

We know from his work that his spirit was kin to exaltation; but we learn from the records of his life that he
was quick to grasp sword, voice turning ugly and provocative, fist clenched for threat or striking; that he was a
scorner of the unlearned, a scholar and blasphemer; but
above all, that he was young: young in life, young in
death—twenty-nine when thrust through the head by a
dagger in a tavern quarrel. In dealing with a poet, however, a chronology of violence may be less biographical
than certain lines—

Where both deliberat, the loue is slight,
Who euer lov'd, that lov'd not at first sight?

For three and a half centuries, men who hated him,
men who worshipped, plodders drawn thither by the
gleam of poetry, have come to Marlowe's shrine and de-
posited their books and pamphlets. To see him clearly
now, it is necessary to beat back through the woods of
words to his own day. Although I am largely indebted

to the research of others, as all must be who turn to the study of Marlowe's life, I cannot help remarking at the start that it is precisely what they failed to do that led me to undertake this biography.

My aim was to bring him and his friends and enemies into focus—first, as men; second, as Elizabethans against the background of their time. It is perhaps possible to write another kind of book about Marlowe; here, the occasionally full accounts of his acquaintances is in accordance with my plan, which was to throw light on his life by showing how his familiars lived, whenever the records dealing exclusively with him seemed inadequate. I have, however, saved my readers the tedium of acquaintance with all the Christopher Marlowes who were not the poet, but whom I have had to meet, albeit under the most erudite auspices. As for the courtlings whose roles may possibly furnish us with a notion of Marlowe's extra-literary activities, I leave them in the shadows from which they were invoked by scholars. Marlowe is our man—we can't have enough of him.

As a matter of fact, it is only when Marlowe is in trouble that we find any trace of him outside his writing. The legal documents concerning him tell much about his character, dramatically supplementing the personality revealed in his work. To quote bits from these, as some have done, with comments pedantic or pontifical, did not seem sufficient, and I have made them the foundation of this work. They tell the story of Marlowe and his dealings as it was told by his contemporaries. Nothing less should satisfy us. It remains to be added that while I have scrupulously adhered to the story found in the records and documents, occasionally, in the accompanying dramatic reconstructions, it has been necessary to go beyond them. No incident, however, has been projected without warrant from the records, and I have not put words into his mouth, with an 'Od's bodikins' to lend verisimilitude.

I take this opportunity of acknowledging the publication of Chapter Four and parts of Chapters Five and Six in *Theatre Arts*. I have also utilized a paragraph or two and several sentences from an article on Marlowe which I wrote for *The Bookman*. Thanks are due to my friends, Mr. Francesco Bianco and Mr. Willard R. Trask, for much useful advice and assistance with translations; to Colonel John Bakeless for generously placing at my disposal photostats of Marlowe documents and some of the illustrations used in this book, and for his kind offer to read the galleys with the following remark, 'that I must read the book some time and may as well do it when I can still be of use;' to Dr. Samuel A. Tannenbaum for many pleasant and fruitful discussions; and to Mr. John S. Lamont, of Rinehart & Co., who prepared the manuscript for the press.

The quotations from Marlowe's work are from Professor Tucker Brooke's *Oxford* edition, and it is his canon that I follow. For those unfamiliar with Elizabethan spelling, it may be useful to point out that the letter 'i' may stand for 'j,' and that 'u' and 'v' are interchangeable.

THE

MUSES' DARLING

CHAPTER I

Poet and Queen

1.

IN the year of Our Lord 1587, Christopher Marlowe, divinity student, ended his school days by wresting an M.A. from Cambridge with the assistance of Elizabeth's Privy Council. He tasted triumph quickly, and its giddiness never left him. The savor of his victory may be found in a boast—

And tis a prety toy to be a Poet—

early in his first play for the London stage.

In 1587, Elizabeth—'la plus fine femme du monde,' as Henry III of France called her, with witty ambiguity —had occupied the throne of England twenty-nine years. She had reached her irascible stage. 'She was of personage tall, of hair and complexion fair, and therewith well favoured, but high nosed, of limbs and features neat, and which added to the lustre of those exteriour Graces, of Stately and Majestick comportment.' Thus Sir Robert Naunton [1] has described her, adding: 'Toward her last she grew hard to please.'

Yet not only the Muses, but the gods as well, had smiled upon her reign, and the god of love was one of their company. Her suitors had all been optimistic; they

3

could not foresee, from the way she played the game, that one day a poet would write,

A most unspotted lily shall she pass
To the ground,

and that it would be the truth, so far as they were concerned. Perhaps what Ben Jonson told Drummond of Hawthornden, however, 'that she had a membrana on her which made her uncapable of man,' had something to do with it.

She was not precisely the paragon one might imagine from all this. She was indecisive and malicious, with all the caprices of a woman who, apparently, was something less or something more. Who can say now what she really was? Her cold eyes look from the splendid portraits, look out and give no sign; but her attire, sown with jewels, the ruffs and frills setting off that plain and sharp countenance, tell something; as does the flattery she accepted as her due from all men—masters of action by land or by sea, and men who could put sweet cadences into the iron English tongue. All did her bidding—the far-famed, laced and jeweled Earl of Leicester bent his ribboned knee to her, her Puritan and practical chief councilor, Sir Francis Walsingham, kept sharp his wits and his wisdom for her and for the realm.

Jonson's gossip from the court poses, perhaps it resolves, the enigma of Elizabeth.

The tragedy of Mary Stuart was past; the ordeal of Essex was in the future. Pending was the Armada. The death of the Scottish Queen had sent ambassadorial pouches pell-mell out of London to stir the courts of Europe, and rumors of war or invasion blew in with the winds from the great ports to the hinterland. In a spider web of plot and counterplot, Elizabeth's Privy Council watched over the realm, its spies in Rome, in Paris, in the Catholic seminary at Rheims, haven of fugitives from Protestant England. At its head was ever-ailing Secretary Walsingham,[2] trim-bearded like a scholar, and with an orange stuck full of cloves pendent from his neck to dispel, with a sniff, the miasmas of plague or hypochondria. His enmity to the Catholic cause went back fifteen years to a night in the Faubourg St. Germain, where he had dwelt as Her Majesty's ambassador. Suddenly the bells of churches began to ring out, thronging the night air with sound, and terrified Englishmen clamored at his door, their faces etched with horror. The Massacre of St. Bartholomew's Eve had begun. He had never forgotten.

The fall of the ax at Fotheringhay had been mainly his doing; he was Mary's implacable foe. But Puritan though he was, his hatred of her had been political, not religious, for he saw in her while she lived a rallying point for the enemies of Elizabeth. For fifteen years, since he had asked to be recalled from Paris, all his influence and machinations had been directed toward Mary's destruction. Now it was over. He had served his royal mistress well. But England's danger was not over. There loomed now, on the horizon of his thoughts, James of Scotland, Philip of Spain, and 'that sweet enemy, France'—his late son-in-law's phrase, Sir Philip Sidney.

2.

It is June's end. Damp ghosts from the Thames haunt the administration building at Westminster where he pores over state papers. Outside, on the busy river, watermen's cries take the air like gulls.

He sits in the Privy Council chamber, mulling over his memories, and smiles benignly at a resolution in the Council minutes, drawn up at a session which he had not attended. Present had been the Lord Archbishop, Lord Chancellor, Lord Treasurer, Lord Chamberlain and Her Majesty's Comptroller; under their joint hands a stern letter had been despatched to the University of Cambridge, and even as Secretary Walsingham reads, a messenger of Her Majesty's Chamber is posting northeast to deliver it:

'Whereas it was reported that Christopher Morley was determined to haue gone beyond the seas to Reames and there to remaine Their Lordships thought good to certefie that he had no such intent but that in all his accons he had behaued him selfe orderlie and discreetelie wherebie he had done her majestie good service, and deserued to be rewarded for his faithfull dealinge: Their Lordships' request was that the rumor thereof should be allaied by all possible meanes, and that he should be furthered in the degree he was to take this next Commencement: Because it was not her majesties pleasure that anie one emploied as he had been in matters touching the benefitt of his Countrie should be defamed by those that are ignorant in th' affaires he went about.'[3]

The Privy Council certifies Marlowe's 'good service'.

What a salutation indeed from the Queen's Majesty, to her humble servant, a poet! All the stories of Marlowe as spy, as a plotter or complotter, stem from the contemporary gossip that prompted the Privy Council to frame this extraordinary document; and from the document itself. The gossip began on the campus of Cambridge, and spilled over into London during Marlowe's absences from the university. The document, unfortunately, is as exasperating as it is intriguing. Their Lordships had no intention of telling any more than they had to in order to make it an effective instrument to crown Marlowe's academic career with a master's degree. They have indeed told as little as possible. No other information has been garnered to supplement or illumine their dark phraseology. What are the probabilities?

Marlowe had absented himself considerably from Corpus Christi College. The gossip was that he went to Rheims, a center of Catholic plots against Elizabeth. Their Lordships state that he did not intend to remain there; if we assume from this that he actually went to Rheims, it was not as a Catholic proselyte that he went. The contrary appears to be true, for the document states by inference that he was back, and unequivocally that 'he had done her majestie good service' in 'matters touching the benefitt of his Countrie.'

What 'good service' was it in his power to do? If he went to Rheims, was it not to the Catholic seminary there? If his role was that of a spy—perhaps 'observer' would be a more approximate word—he would have been welcomed in his divinity student's gown.

Their Lordships are at pains to distinguish his behavior as orderly and discreet; given a mission of some importance to accomplish, he had accomplished it satisfactorily. Perhaps in addition to going to Rheims, Marlowe had been instructed to indicate papist predilections to his fellow divinity students, in which case reports of his leanings would have preceded him abroad, to smooth the way. This would sufficiently account for the necessity of an official denial afterwards. Marlowe's table talk, it was reported against him later, praised Catholic ritual and may date from this period: 'That if there be any god or any good Religion, then it is in the Papistes because the service of god is performed with more Cerimonies, as Elevation of the mass, organs, singing men, Shaven Crownes & cta. That all protestantes are Hypocriticall asses.'

It is even possible that Marlowe did not go abroad at all, but, after stating his own position, falsely, merely acted as an informer on those who confided in him their supposedly mutual sympathies. I do not choose to accept this last view, but I give it. If this was so, in mitigation it might be said that those who planned to join the Catholic nestlings at Rheims or Rome were traitors to their government and their school, and being double-dealers themselves, merited double-dealing.

One other point might be noted. Whether Marlowe went to Rheims or not, he was able to observe, at first hand, political intrigue cloaked by religion—orthodoxy as a device of policy and the servants of God flouting the divine laws of conduct—to ripen his cynicism early.

CHAPTER II

A Pattern for Conflict

I.

THE road taken by Christopher Marlowe to the high places of London is dark, but here and there along the way a sudden lantern lights up a surmise. Considering his beginnings and his end, his life appears as a pattern for conflict; but perhaps this can be said of any life. Those who find significance in violent contrasts will no doubt observe that his bold thought and rebellious spirit emerged from an atmosphere of unruffled sanctity.

In 1540, Christopher Marley, tanner, of the parish of Westgate, Canterbury, bequeathed his soul to God and all the company of heaven, leaving money and lands to his wife Joan; and 'to the child that she goyth with all if hitt be a man child,' two houses, together with furniture and hangings, and some additional land. This posthumous child and heir, who was named John, is believed to have been the father of Christopher Marlowe, and there is much to bolster such a belief. He wrote his name as Marley all his life; he was apprenticed to a shoemaker, which was natural for the son of a tanner, and he became a shoemaker himself. In 1561, when he was twenty-one years old, he married Catherine Arthur, presumably the daughter of Christopher Arthur, sometime rector of St. Peter's,

Canterbury. The poet, therefore, was named for either of his grandfathers, or for both.

Christopher Marlowe was born on or about February 26, 1564, two months before Shakespeare. The first definite record of his life appears in the register of St. George the Martyr, near St. George's Gate, the church in which his parents were married:

> The 26ᵗʰ day of ffebruary was Christened
> Christofer the sonne of John Marlow.

He was the Marlowes' second child, the first having been a girl who did not survive the rigors of an Elizabethan upbringing. The February 6 birth-date given by some writers has no satisfactory explanation. If he was a healthy baby, he probably was baptized several days after birth, according to custom; but if sickly, he would have been rushed to the baptismal font.

The house he was born in—according to Canterbury tradition—still stands, on the corner of St. George's Street and St. George's Lane.[a] Down the street is the church, with its baptismal font still in use. The house, half-timbered, and dating unquestionably from the age of Elizabeth, was once replete with carved oaken panels, long since torn out. The second story overhangs the lane. Over all is a gabled attic. The wills of the Marlowe womenfolk reveal it was a house full of little treasuries of gold and silver rings, silver tableware, wall hangings, and great heaps of sheets and napkins, smocks and petticoats.

[a] Now reported blitzed.

'The Cittie of Canterbury is a fayre & large Citty, well walled': the West Gate with a view of the past.

The birthplace of Christopher Marlowe according to Canterbury tradition: back and side as in Elizabeth's day.

No other male child of the Marlowes lived for long, and Christopher's boyhood was spent in a house with four sisters, all younger than himself. Jane and Anne married shoemakers; Dorothy, a vintner, and Margaret a tailor. Jane's husband, John Moore, is of further interest to us, and will reappear.

2.

To call Marlowe's father a 'shoemaker' with its modern connotations is misleading. Two months after the christening of his son, John Marlowe became a freeman of the city of Canterbury by apprenticeship. Freemen controlled trade, since only members of a guild could start a new business. This he now did, becoming a member of the Brethren of the Assumption of Our Lady, of the Crafts and Mysteries of Shoe-Makers, Coriours and Cobbelers—the shoemakers' guild.

This was for him the start of a long and prosperous career as a Canterbury business man, respectable and respected in the community; and he begins almost at once to appear in court records as a bearer of tidings or testimony that carried weight. At about the time his son Christopher was born, he deposed a year later in a libel suit, he heard the following derogatory remark about a townswoman from Lawrence Applegate, a tailor: 'I haue hadd my pleasure of godlyve Chappmans Daughter.'

Something of John Marlowe's pious indignation upon hearing this can be felt from the rest of his deposition: 'that diuers tymes syns and in sondrie places the said Lawrence Applegate hath most sclanderouslie affirmed the foresaid wordes and in repeting and acknoledging the same wold say that godwiff Chapman didd owe vnto hym the same Lawrence twoo shillinges and quoth he she wold nott pay me the said twoo shillings but retayned & kepte back the same for that I occupyed godliff hir Daughter fower times which was for everie tyme vj pence.'

Such was life in the cathedral city of Canterbury in the spring of 1564.

While Christopher was growing up and learning to read and write, probably in a parochial classroom, his father, with apprentices of his own, expanded his business; his family grew larger. At length, in 1573, when Christopher was in his tenth year, John Marlowe, seeking larger quarters, removed from St. George's parish to the center of the city. There, in St. Andrew's parish, the last of his children was born; and in memory of another Marlowe baby briefly in this world he was christened Thomas. Like the first Thomas, however, he also died young. By the time Christopher was fifteen his father had begun to act as a bondsman for couples seeking marriage licenses—a tribute, perhaps, to his standing as a prosperous business man who was also the son-in-law of a churchman. As a matter of fact, John Marlowe himself had an odor of sanctity about him, for he became a churchwarden and died a parish clerk.

It is not surprising that in the eyes of his family Christopher was marked for the church. The rule was an old one—State for gentry, Church for the poor man's son—poor, that is, in contrast to hereditary riches or hereditary pride. On January 14, 1579, Christopher Marlowe entered King's School, Canterbury, on one of fifty scholarships maintained there for boys between the ages of nine and fifteen—the years of the treble or boy soprano—with minds 'apt for learning.' One pound, eight shillings and four pence was the annual stipend of a King's scholar, to which was added an allowance for commons, i.e., food, and money for two and a half yards of cloth for a new gown every Christmas. This was skimpy, or the boys were kept lean in their devotions.

A few weeks short of being fifteen, Marlowe was just under the age limit for admission. Physically and spiritually the school snuggled close to the cathedral where Thomas à Becket fell a martyr. Piety and Latin made up the curriculum, and a responsive psalm began and ended the day. Belled in his gown, he went punctually to and fro from St. Andrew's, past the Rush Market, the Bishop's palace, and almost to the city's walls, storing his mind with magnificent, medieval images—the towers, streets and streams of Canterbury; churches at dusk blazing like jewels, and priories and friaries standing watch at the outposts of the city—and remembering forever, from the age of nine, the pomp and pageantry of Queen Elizabeth's progress to Archbishop Parker's abode.

Left to himself, he might have trod simpler paths than those he was to follow; but prodded and pushed to the magnificent portals of the *Ecclesia Anglicana,* he at length rebelled.

CHAPTER III

Divinity Student into Poet

I.

IN DECEMBER, 1580, when he was seventeen years old, and perhaps already somewhat alert to the foibles of the religious after two years at King's School, Christopher Marlowe presented himself to the authorities at Cambridge, holding a nomination to a scholarship in Corpus Christi College. It was one of several created by the will of Archbishop Parker of Canterbury, who believed in helping young men to don the cloth, and who had a precise and practical mind to make it feasible: '*Item*, I wish my Executors to make ready a chamber in that college, now called *A Storehouse*, for three other of my scholars to inhabit, for each of which I wish three pounds, six shillings and eight pence to be given annually in the form which my Executors shall prescribe in writing. Of which scholars I wish the first to be chosen from Canterbury (i.e., King's) School, and to be a native of that place.' [1]

Parker's son, John, made it even more specific when he took charge of the will after his father's death (and contributes, incidentally, some additional strokes to the never-to-be-completed portrait of Marlowe): 'All which said schollers shall and must at the time of their election be so entred into the skill of song as that they shall at

14

the first sight solf and sing plaine song. And that they shalbe of the best and aptest schollers well instructed in their gramer and if it may be such as can make a verse.' There is, unfortunately, no way of telling how Marlowe stood up as a singer in meeting these specifications—probably adequately; but if he did not already know how to make a verse, he learned fast.

Thus a ground floor chamber, previously used for storage, became the dwelling place of Marlowe for more than a fifth of his life. There he lived six years, gathering the slow, somber harvest of disillusionment.

In 1581, the colleges of Cambridge numbered some 1,862 students, and salted among them 'an hundred preachers at the least, very worthy men,' as a report to Parliament stated. Many of the students subsisted on the slimmest kind of fare in pursuit of their studies, rising at four in the morning, joining in prayers for an hour, then plunging into private study or common lectures until nightfall, when some of them were 'fayne to walk or runne vp and down halfe an houre, to gette a heate on their feete whan they go to bed.' Strictly-enforced regulations provided 'that no scholler doe weare any long lockes of Hayre uppon his heade, but that he be polled, notted, or rounded,' and that 'no scholler shall weare any Barilled Hosen' or 'great Ruffs.' In such an atmosphere a young man with Marlowe's temperament would be confronted almost at once with the disconcerting realization that holy orders were not for him.

Yet, despite the oppressive ecclesiastical atmosphere and discipline, Cambridge was a very place 'of nestling green for Poets made,' and it was the right place for Marlowe. An illustrious procession of names great in English literature had issued thence; the last, and perhaps the most inspiring, was that of Edmund Spenser, 'the new Poete.' It was here, too, probably, that Marlowe first made the acquaintance of two men whose names are forever associated with his as friend and envious foe of his London days: Thomas Nashe, who was in residence from 1582 to 1586, when he took his B.A., going no further; and Robert Greene, who was a B.A. of 1580, an M.A. of 1584, and who took an M.A. at Oxford as well, as he liked to boast.

On library shelves were the materials for Marlowe's first and last great dramatic works: the *Theatrum Orbis Terrarum* of the geographer Ortelius; Pedro Mexia's *Silva de varia lección*, Englished as *The Foreste* by Thomas Fortescue, with a bibliography which Marlowe diligently pursued in the writing of *Tamburlaine*; and *Holinshed*, chief source of *Edward II*. There were also the classic poets; and plays, written and produced by Cambridge students.

By the time Nashe and Greene had begun to live the lives of struggling authors in the metropolis, Marlowe was prepared to speed after them. He galloped by way of Westminster and the opulent suburbs. For somewhere along the road to being ordained, he attracted attention to himself as something more than just another candidate for holy orders. Resident at Cambridge while Marlowe was a student there was Robert Cecil, son of Lord Burghley, the Lord Treasurer of England and Chancellor of the university. Past this bare linking of their names lies the sequel in the half-Protestant, half-Catholic world of Mary Queen of Scots and Elizabeth, a sequel of service for the state which Burghley helped to reward. It is impossible to tell now how the poet was drawn into the politico-religious drama of his time. The hunchbacked, intellectual Cecil, if this is in truth the explanation, would have been one to admire Marlowe, robust in word and deed.

2.

In addition to future statesmen and fledgling poets in the anonymous host of apprentice divines, there was present at Cambridge a Puritan of a sharp countenance, Gabriel Harvey, Fellow of Pembroke Hall.

Harvey, renowned as a rhetorician and orator, was one of the notable figures at the university, respectfully pointed out to newcomers as the friend of Edmund Spenser, now a decade out of Cambridge. It was through Harvey's acquaintance with Sir Philip Sidney and the Earl of Leicester that Spenser had found preferment, first as private secretary to Arthur Lord Grey of Wilton, Elizabeth's Lord Deputy in Ireland where, amid the cruelty and carnage of the Anglo-Irish wars, the murmurous, multitudinous stanzas of *The Faerie Queene* poured forth, canto after canto, book after book, to be forever talked about and, save by poets, little read.

A man acquainted at court; a classical scholar who stood high in the select circles of Cambridge's intellectual and theological leaders; the friend of a poet whose fame was growing; discreet, stern; withal sure of himself, whether at cards or discourse in the houses of the local gentry, dazzling the womenfolk with his learning when he was not charming them with his manners, Harvey went about with the air of an Olympian that

> like a looker-on
> Of this worldes stage, doest note with critique pen,
> The sharp dislikes of each condition.

Thus Spenser characterized his 'singular good frend' Harvey, writing to him from Dublin, in a sonnet which the schoolman was to publish, out of vanity, just as he had previously published a little book of their correspondence: *Three Proper, and wittie, familiar Letters: lately passed betvvene tvvo Vniuersitie men: touching the Earthquake in Aprill last, and our English refourmed Versifying*—two of his letters to Spenser's one, both full of learned jests at which only pedants can smile; one replete with an account of what Harvey told his host and hostess and their other guests of an evening in April when an earth tremor shook the house, question and answer and finally discourse in which Harvey took the floor to deliver what he termed a 'short, but sharpe, and learned Iudgement of Earthquakes,' recalling each detail and turn of phrase, for he had shone, and his own light still dazzled him; and in the other setting forth his opinions about prosody, with samples. Like many scholars of the time, Harvey believed that English poetry should follow classical prosody, pre-

ferring the hexameter—in English a dull measure: tee-
dum, tee-dum, tee-dum, tee-dum, tee-dum, tee-dum—to
rhymed lines, and seeking to influence Spenser in that direction. Spenser's mellifluously cadenced and rhymed
stanzas were the poet's reply to the pedant.

Harvey never got over the pleasures of print. Beginning with these publications, his name linked to Spenser's
forever, he took up his 'critique pen' whenever an opportunity offered. He will show, in the course of this book,
into what black depths the pen of a scholar and gentleman
can be dipped.

Be that as it may, when Marlowe came along at Cambridge, the contrast between the gentle, unassuming poet
Harvey had known and the newcomer must have been too
startling, too disconcerting. Perhaps an explanation lies in
the fact that Harvey, as a deputy proctor, had the power
to punish minor offenses. Marlowe may have collided
with him. Greene and Nashe may have done likewise.

Harvey, son of a rope-maker at Saffron Walden, a village near Cambridge, had two brothers—John, who became an astronomer and 'phisition,' and Richard, who left
Cambridge in 1586, a year before Marlowe, to become
rector of Chislehurst, in Kent, the parish of Thomas Walsingham, kinsman of Elizabeth's chief councilor. Richard
Harvey seems also to have met up with the poet, as we
shall see.

3.

To Marlowe, apparently, the life of a divinity student,
with its shilling a week and pleasure shunned, was for a

martyr or a dolt, and he was neither. He had been hurried past the sun-bright world of men and women into the chapel glooms of prayer, the grays of disputation, by doting parents, helpful friends, and routine carried him along. Native wit made him a tolerable scholar. He was also a tolerable resident, even as regards piety in its outward manifestations, so often violent, for there is no record of a clash with any of his roommates. As for his studies—rhetoric, dialectic, philosophy—he was neither at the top nor the bottom of the list of candidates for a B.A.

In the spring of 1584, when he was twenty years old, we find him making his *supplicat* for the degree of Bachelor of Arts, the first great reward for interminable prayers, study and lectures: 'Christopher Marlin petitions that the twelve completed terms in which he has followed the ordinary lectures (even if not wholly according to the forms of the statute), together with all the opponencies, responsions and other exercises required by royal statute, may suffice for him to take the examination,' and plain 'Marlin' became 'Dominus Marlin.' (The phrase in parenthesis—'even if not wholly according to the forms of the statute'—occurs in other *supplicats*, and is not significant.)

The degree marked progress of a sort, but with it came restrictions that must have been irksome. He could no longer venture abroad into the pleasant streets of Cambridge without a gown of 'sad color' to his ankles and a standing hood, for statute required that the dignity of graduates be maintained; and before him lay the somber vista of three more years of prayer, study and lectures, with the additional subjects of perspective, astronomy (in which he might have delighted), Greek, and more philosophy, for his Master of Arts and ordination. Now if his heart had been in it, he could have proceeded to make a place for himself as a rural religious, assured of a living, as his roommates were to do. His heart was not. To add to his anguish, he was a poet. What else he was, or appeared to be, his enemies, in time, will relate. He read much that was not in the curriculum, and occasionally hied himself off on business of his own, leaving sizeable gaps in the records of his residence. Doubt took the city of his mind. Later, in the story of another divinity student who turned from the church he put it into words:

> Settle thy studies, *Faustus,* and beginne
> To sound the deapth of that thou wilt professe:
> Hauing commencde, be a Diuine in shew—

but he himself could not; and doubt joined with cynicism as he observed his fellows piously striding toward the pulpit and earthly security, their hands firmly upon two worlds, and an aura about them of blandness and belief which he did not desire and could not envy. In a weaker character, less compact of ardor and intellect, it might have been disastrous; in Marlowe it bore bright but sometimes bitter fruit:

> I do repent, and yet I do dispaire:
> Hell striues with grace for conquest in my breast,
> What shal I do to shun the snares of death?

Perhaps these autobiographical lines were conceived, in their first form at least, during this period of inner conflict at Cambridge. The passage is steeped in an anguish which we can feel even if the emotion was recollected in tranquillity.

But even before *Doctor Faustus* the process of evaluation, of self-probing and self-torture, had gone on—his years in Cambridge, except for rare periods of creation, could not have been happy ones. The production of *Tamburlaine* followed so fast upon his arrival in London, that we may assume that at least a portion of it was conceived or written at Corpus Christi, in the storehouse converted into an apartment for scholars by Archbishop Parker's bequest. *Tamburlaine* is strewn with the dead faith and derision of a divinity student who found Christianity unpalatable and repugnant, and who discovered in poetry, and indeed in the whole pagan past of the world, spiritual comfort and inspiration. The ritualistic trappings of a religion that was in at the birth and death of every Englishman, of a church that governed the souls of men with temporal policies and power—these he rejected; and he rejected them as a writer must, for the whole world to mark, in his writing.

What, then, did he believe? It is too constant in his work to be denied—in a Supreme Being; or, if this was not so, his earliest training had left such an impress on his mind that the belief came up unconsciously, itself a form of belief; for he salutes in heaven the deity of his Biblical studies—

The chiefest God first moouer of that Spheare,
Enchac'd with thousands euer shining lamps—

the monotheistic God of the Hebrews,

full of reuenging wrath,
From whom the thunder and the lightning breaks;

and reiterates for men's guidance the Old Testament truth,

That Vertue solely is the sum of glorie.

Over and over the image of

The God that sits in heauen, if any God,
For he is God alone, and none but he,

and a personal morality caught up from his studies, to be confirmed by observation, stand forth in his work. The Old Testament is a source book from which he drew throughout his career.

His mind aspired to the firmament; its stars and splendor light up his pages. The doubt which undermined his faith turned to a worship of God's world, where

Flora in her mornings pride,
Shaking her siluer tresses in the aire,
Rain'st on the earth resolued pearle in showers—

a world of beauty without the dubious exegesis of men. He
appears to have undergone a continual struggle to believe,
but his faith had to contend, at every step, with what he
saw. His faith faltered. He turned to worship at another
shrine,

> Wher Beauty, mother to the Muses sits.

4.

I see him alone there, in the room that had been a
storehouse, with the books that he kept hidden from his
roommates, books that were his own little storehouses of
delight, his 'infinite riches in a little roome,' as he was to
write later.

His life, up to this time, had been for the most part a
cloistered one; he had breathed, till he had revolted, the
odor of sanctity; but in secret moments and hours he had
snatched the sweets of poetry from Ovid and Virgil;
heard, in the still, monastic nights, renown's music rising
from their pages. Ovid, in particular, was full of stolen
delights; exultingly he turns to his translations, already
for him the auguries of a way of life that offered more
than the cold aisles of churches and incantations without
joy:

> Let base conceipted witts admire vilde things,
> Faire *Phoebus* lead me to the Muses springs.
> About my head be quiuering mirtle wound,
> And in sad louers heads let me be found.

(Years later, writing the dedication for a friend's post-humous poems, the myrtle of Venus, sown throughout Ovid's verses, recurred to him.) It is difficult to believe that anyone could ever have adopted a condescending attitude towards Marlowe's translations, but that is the case in the pedantic world:

> Now in her tender armes I sweetly bide,
> If euer, now well lies she by my side.
> The aire is cold, and sleepe is sweetest now
> And birdes send forth shrill notes from euery bough.

In little, Ovid's *Amores* reiterated the subject matter for a love poem, and Marlowe steeped himself in their sensuousness, while developing an idiom of his own:

> Loe I confesse, I am thy captiue I,
> And holde my conquer'd hands for thee to tie.

And from the Latin poet's ever-recurring image of a naked girl by the bedside came, at length, that burst of glory that lights the ending of *Hero and Leander* (Marlowe's ending, of course; not Chapman's):

> Thus neere the bed she blushing stood vpright,
> And from her countenance behold ye might
> A kind of twilight breake . . . .

This was the beginning—to be stirred by the splendor of timeless lines and the dignity of great and lonely

achievement. But Ovid had been full of other matters
besides young love and the high functions of poetry. Now,
as Marlowe fumbles through his papers, exulting in
snatches, he comes upon passages whose thoughts had
helped to shape his own, which had given form to his
misgivings, and comforted his loneliness, pent in the
monastic walls of the university:

> God is a name, no substance, feard in vaine,
> And doth the world in fond beliefe deteine.

The authorities were going after heresy with fire and
iron, stake and rack. A fellow of Corpus Christi was actually burnt at the stake for holding that Christ was not
God, but would be 'made God after his second resurra-
tion.' Atheism was equally dangerous, even for the dab-
bler. But only simpletons got into trouble:

> The gods care we are cald, and men of piety,
> And some there be that thinke we haue a deity.

Not Ovid; what of himself? He was never sure; faith
and doubt alternated in his breast, as his own work bears
witness.

Marlowe's renderings from Ovid are not the work of
a skilled translator. They are not accurate, but they are
not dull. He has shown them to a select few, and they
passed from hand to hand as students greeted each other
solemnly on the quad or in the dim-lit passageways of the
great halls of learning:

Weake Elegies, delightful Muse farewell;
A worke, that after my death, heere shall dwell.

One newly-arrived Corpus Christi student 'learnd all
Marlo by heart.' He was still in Cambridge when *Dr.
Faustus* was produced in London, and full of worshipful
zeal for Marlowe, or just plain daft, tried to conjure the
devil, but was confronted instead by irate dons. As for
Marlowe's translations from Ovid when they were finally
published, the book containing them was ordered publicly
burned by the Archbishop of Canterbury and the Bishop of
London.

5.

In addition to poetry, he found relief in action. How
else are we to account for his strange record of attendance,
or the lack of it, at Corpus Christi?

Despite the wording of Archbishop Parker's bequest,
his scholars were paid as were the holders of other scholarships at Cambridge, that is, one shilling a week while in
residence. Thus, from the extant college Audits, it is possible to tell how long Marlowe was in residence in any
given term. During the academic year 1584-85, after taking his B.A., he seems to have been absent more than half
the time. The audits are missing for 1585-86, but the college Buttery accounts show him making purchases of food
consistently, except for two weeks in November. In
March, however, he disappears from the Buttery Book,
and does not reappear until June. For the academic year

1586-87, the latter his last, he seems to have been present for only a part of the first term and part of the second—nine weeks, and five and a half weeks, respectively, as shown by the entries of payments to him. His name is omitted altogether for the third and four terms, and when a new scholar was enrolled for the scholarship Marlowe held, the poet's name was left out, as though in punishment for some offense, although it was customary to designate the old with the new holder.

Marlowe's attendance record is unusual, particularly as he was graduated with an M.A.—although he had to fight for it, which is not surprising. Where did he go when he was not at Corpus Christi? What did he do?

Two records provide evidence of his whereabouts on at least two of his absences. The first is the Privy Council's letter to the university, which memorializes his services to the state. The second is somewhat less spectacular.

During his fortnight's disappearance in the latter half of November, 1585, he apparently was in Canterbury, where he helped perform a neighborly office. With his father, John Marlowe; his brother-in-law John Moore, and a Thomas Arthur, perhaps his uncle, Christopher Marlowe witnessed a will. As his signature on this will is unique, and as the surrounding signatures make it impossible to doubt its authenticity, the circumstances may prove interesting in detail.[2]

The will witnessed by the Marlowes and their kin was that of a Catherine Benchkin of St. Michael's parish. The will was proved a year later, and John Marlowe was summoned to testify concerning it. Under the date October 5,

1586, he recalled that the witnessing took place 'aboute a twelmonethes agon,' and then deposed as follows: 'he this deponent, beeing requested by John Benchkin to come to the howse of his mother Catherine Benchkin scituat in St Michaels parishe in Canterburye went thither accompanied with Thomas Arthur his precontest and coming thether they fownde there this deponentes Soonne Christofer Marley and John Moore, this deponentes Soonne in Lawe and Preconteste, and beeing there altogether the testatrix Catherine Benchkin towlde them that she had sent for them to bee witnesses to her will.'

'Precontest' means a previous witness, for the old woman had made an earlier will. When she showed them the new will, John Marlowe related, 'this deponentes Soonne requested him to reade the same which beeing by him soe read the saide testatrix acknowledged the same to bee her laste will and testament, and alsoe Caste into the ffire one other owlde will which she said she had beefore tyme made.' The witnesses thereupon subscribed their signatures in the following order:

John Marley
Thomas Arthur
Christofer Marley
John Moore

It is worth noting that the poet here spells his name precisely like his father, who signed himself Marley consistently.

Despite the solemnity of the occasion, it is a pleasant,

Prayer by the Hour-Glass

if fleeting, glimpse of Marlowe in the bosom of his family. We get no other. At one end of the city, past St. Dunstan's, lay the road to London; at the other, through Dover Lane, past the Nunnery, lay the road to Dover, only sixteen miles away. We know now that he may have used either exit; but this time his absence from Cambridge was brief, for two weeks later he was back.

6.

He prayed and studied, studied and prayed, read the classics, and wrote verse. The amount of writing he did at Corpus is remarkable, even for that prolific age; for to this period, besides his translations of Ovid, must be assigned a line-for-line translation of the first book of Lucan's *Pharsalia*, wherein he switched from rhymed lines to blank verse, never to return except for the brief and beautiful 'Come Live With Me' and *Hero and Leander*. His version of Lucan in blank verse is one of the earliest poems in English in that medium. It influenced poets from Milton to Wordsworth, for it marks the first weaving into English poetry of foreign place-names, and a first philosophical contemplation of nature, as these lines taken at random show:

> As when against pine bearing *Ossa's* rocks
> Beates *Thracian Boreas;* or when trees bow downe,
> And rustling swing . . .

and

> that vncertaine shore,
> Which is nor sea, nor land, but oft times both,
> And changeth as the Ocean ebbes and flowes.

He gave both Milton and Wordsworth images and rhythms ready-made to their hands.

With Lucan we begin to get a preview of Marlowe's later imagery and music, as in this passage (which might apply equally to the uncertainties of this atomic age):

> But *Figulus* more seene in heauenly mysteries,
> Whose like *Aegiptian Memphis* neuer had
> For skill in stars, and tune-full planeting,
> In this sort spake: The worlds swift course is lawlesse
> And casuall; all the starres at randome range:
> Or if *Fate* rule them, Rome thy Cittizens

Are neere some plague: what mischiefe shall insue?
Shall townes be swallowed? shall the thickned aire,
Become intemperate? shall the earth be barraine?
Shall water be conieal'd and turn'd to ice?
O Gods what death prepare ye? with what plague
Meane ye to radge? the death of many men
Meetes in one period.

But Lucan was merely preparation for something
greater. With Lucan out of the way, he turned for the
first time to drama—his medium, blank verse.

Plays with classical themes had been performed at
Cambridge, and it was perhaps inevitable that Marlowe
should try his 'prentice hand on a classical subject. Virgil
provided the material; it is almost all Virgil's *Aeneid* in
The Tragedie of Dido Queene of Carthage.

Dido contains, in tentative form, all that delights us in
Marlowe. The bright images, 'mighty' lines and sensuous
passages of the later plays are here in, as it were, a first
draft:

O here he comes, loue, loue, giue *Dido* leaue
To be more modest then her thoughts admit,
Lest I be made a wonder to the world.

'Come Live With Me' is foreshadowed:

Ile giue thee tackling made of riueld gold,
Wound on the barkes of odoriferous trees,
Oares of massie Iuorie full of holes,

Through which the water shall delight to play:
Thy Anchors shall be hewed from Christall Rockes,
Which if thou lose shall shine aboue the waues;

as is the great scene in *Doctor Faustus:*

Not bloudie speares appearing in the ayre,
Presage the downfall of my Emperie,
Nor blazing Commets threatens *Didos* death,
It is *Aeneas* frowne that ends my daies:
If he forsake me not, I neuer dye,
For in his lookes I see eternitie,
And heele make me immortall with a kisse.

Dido was a storehouse from which Marlowe drew riches until he died; and not only Marlowe. Shakespeare praised it in Hamlet's speech to the players as 'an excellent play, well digested in the scenes, set down with as much modesty as cunning.' But 'it pleased not the million.' It was acted at least once, for the title-page of *Dido* states that it was 'Played by the Children of Her Maiesties Chappell,' who, in May, 1587, when Marlowe's degree hung in the balance, were performing at Norwich and Ipswich, close enough to Cambridge for an aspiring playwright to journey thither with his manuscript. Perhaps this accounts for one of his absences from the university.

Two autobiographical passages should be noted. One appears to be a gibe at Gabriel Harvey; perhaps after a first and disagreeable encounter, Harvey made an attempt at friendship, which failed:

> This was an Orator, and thought by wordes
> To compasse me, but yet he was deceiu'd.

If, as a result of the rebuff recorded here, some harsh things were said, Marlowe answered further:

> Tut, I am simple, without mind to hurt,
> And haue no gall at all to grieue my foes.

Unfortunately, he changed.

With *Dido* out of the way,[3] Marlowe stood on the threshold of his greatest achievements; perhaps he now began to draft *Tamburlaine*.

7.

It is an axiom of the artistic world that no creator ever begins without borrowings. That is his homage to the master or masters whom he follows. There is, as a rule, in his first expression, a strain within a strain, a mingling of predecessor and self, that disarms and charms. Occasionally, it points the way. The artist begins in loneliness, but he finds his affinities before long in other artists, and he models himself accordingly. Afterwards, it is another matter.

In Marlowe's case, we are confronted by the exception. At the very beginning of his career we see him bringing to his work a quality never found before in English verse, a breathless and dramatic lyricism that is all but edged with flame as we read it for the first time; if we choose an

example from his school-day writings, we see it is already
there:

> Then he vnlockt the Horse, and suddenly
> From out his entrailes, *Neoptolemus*
> Setting his speare vpon the ground, leapt forth,
> And after him a thousand Grecians more;
> In whose sterne faces shin'd the quenchles fire,
> That after burnt the pride of *Asia*—

it is Aeneas telling Dido how Troy fell. The iambics
march inexorably to the end of the line, where they stop
abruptly—it was later that Marlowe developed the run-on
line and subtler rhythms—but his youthful, original quality is there for all to mark; it is there from first to last.

Even without the contrast of Marlowe's influence on
his followers, including Shakespeare—especially Shakespeare—the impact of other writers on him is negligible,
without trace. Nevertheless, it was his reading that showed
him the path to follow; but it was only the form, not the
substance, of what he read that impressed him.

Four works at Cambridge could have shown him the
potentialities of blank verse; a fifth, when he reached
London, confirmed them. In the order of time—

Forty years before, two young men had wrought a
reformation in English verse by restoring to it some of
the naturalness it had once possessed. They were the ill-
fated Henry Howard, Earl of Surrey, and his friend, Sir
Thomas Wyatt. Wyatt was the better poet, but Surrey
has had the more lasting influence—indeed, it is a fabulous

subject, this one of pondering the direction English poetry might have taken had he not, in translating two books of the *Aeneid*, used blank verse instead of rhyme. The pedantries of this subject are many and perhaps complex; it may suffice here to say that Surrey's blank verse is either the first example of this medium in English, or merely one of the first; if the latter, his superiority as a poet helped it to survive where others, if others there were, perished. Aeneas's speech to Dido in Surrey's version of Book Two, the fateful dialogue between Aeneas and Dido in Book Four, showed the dramatic possibilities of the five-foot line unencumbered by rhyming words.

The first to avail himself of the new medium for dramatic purposes—once more I put pedantries aside—was Thomas Sackville, Lord Buckhurst, whose *Tragedie of Ferrex and Porrex* was presented, with Queen Elizabeth as a spectator, 'the xviii. day of Janvarie 1561. by the Gentlemen of the Inner Temple.' It was Lord Buckhurst who carried the death warrant to Mary Queen of Scots at Fotheringhay. The *Tragedie of Ferrex and Porrex* is generally believed to have been the first blank verse tragedy in English; perhaps it was only the first good one.

The next considerable blank verse play is *Jocasta*, 'translated and digested into Acte' from the Greek of Euripides 'by George Gascoygne and Francis Kinwelmershe of Grayes Inne, and there by them presented, 1566.' The play was reissued in *The Pleasauntest Workes of George Gascoigne* in 1587, the year of Marlowe's arrival in London. Gascoigne was a good poet, though not read now, and it is interesting to note that he was a Cambridge man and that his patron was Arthur, Lord Grey of Wilton, the employer and patron of Spenser. In view of the charges that were to be brought against Marlowe, it is also interesting to see that similar ones had been lodged against Gascoigne in 1572:

'Item he is a defamed person and noted aswell for manslaughter as for other greate cryemes.

'Item he is a common Rymer and a deviser of slaunderous Pasquelles againste divers personnes of great callinge.

'Item he is a notorious Ruffiaune and especiallie noted to be bothe a Spie, an Atheist and a Godlesse personne.'

We have dealt thus far with gentlemen, more or less, and poets, not professional playwrights. In 1584, George Peele's *Arraignment of Paris* was acted before Queen Elizabeth by the Children of her Chapel. It was published the same year. In it, the old and new forms met—a last contention.

When, finally, Marlowe came to London, he may have seen Thomas Kyd's *Spanish Tragedie* on the stage—it is a question whether *Tamburlaine* or the sensational work by Kyd was produced first.

These were the men, and those the works, that determined the course of English dramatic writing and gave Shakespeare his medium. The issue might have been in doubt before Marlowe arrived on the scene; it never was afterwards. He found an instrument that had served scholarly-minded men, and left it sensitive to the expression of the subtlest mind of all. How far the language had freed itself, and the vitality he brought to it, can be seen by comparing Surrey's version of a passage from the *Aeneid* with Marlowe's:

> Faithless! forsworn! ne Goddess was thy dam!
> Nor Dardanus beginner of thy race!
> But of hard rocks mount Caucase monstruous
> Bred thee, and teats of Tyger gaue thee suck.

Thus Surrey; and thus Marlowe:

> Thy mother was no Goddesse periured man,
> Nor *Dardanus* the author of thy stocke:
> But thou art sprung from *Scythian Caucasus*,
> And Tygers of *Hircania* gaue thee sucke.[4]

8.

He must have known by now that he would never be ordained; but perhaps he knew the value of an M.A. from Cambridge, for authors who might have been sufficiently proud of their literary attainments alone did not hesitate to set forth their scholastic honors on the title-pages of their works.

On 31 March 1587, after six years at Cambridge, Marlowe made his final *supplicat* to the Master and Fellows of Corpus: 'Christopher Marley petitions your reverences that the nine full terms (after his completing the last) in which he has followed the ordinary lectures (even if not wholly in accordance with the form of the statute), together with all the opponencies, responsions and the other exercises required by royal statute, may suffice for him to commence in arts.'

He waited confidently for his *supplicat* to take effect. Or perhaps he disappeared again. Whatever it was, the dons decided that Marlowe was not a fit person to write M.A. from Cambridge after his name. In rage, he turned to the Privy Council for assistance. . . .

In a ground floor chamber in the angle formed by the Old Court at Corpus Christi he waited, hearing in his mind the beat of a horse's hoofs on the highway. Although there were books in the chamber, and not all of them were schoolbooks, he cannot beguile the time by reading as he harks inwardly to the gallop of a horseman along the highway of his thoughts.

In a whirl of images he saw it all—the gowned students whispering together; rumor, like the watchman, making its rounds. He was sick of their holier-than-thou airs, their shuffling, slippered, pious tread; their fulsome obeisance and ceremony; their mincing and waddling, thumbs in belt, eyes to the pavement or rolling towards the sky, embryo divines in the service of a God whose heavens were hung with black. He recalled the raised eyebrow, the quizzical or treacherous look as he aired unorthodox views in sly-earnest debate, making them squirm with his praise of papists. How his tongue had wagged! Words spoken in jest or gibe took on verisimilitude. He had gone to Rheims, said some; he had gone to Rome, said others. The lines of a student play epitomized it:

To Rome or Rhems I'le hye, led on by fate,
Where I will ende my dayes or mende my state,

with its barb for sudden conversions. And he saw the outraged dons hearing all, comprehending all, their faces drawn and stern. Ireful were the dons, for they were the servants of the Lord.

Suddenly the Privy Council's pleasure is made known to them and him; in conclave assembled the Master and Fellows of Corpus Christi peruse their Lordships' commandment, and amazement lights up the faces of shrivelled parchment.

9.

In London in the same year, perhaps at the same time (for thus are writers constantly harried), Thomas Lodge recklessly ran up a bill for seven pounds with one Richard Topping, a tailor of the Strand. Master Topping tried to collect his money, making—no doubt—the usual animadversions touching authors. Then he lost patience and brought an action against Lodge, with the result that the original sum was increased to twelve pounds, which is what happens to debtors who are taken to court, and Lodge himself was placed in the Clink.[5]

From start to finish it was different with Marlowe. There is nothing in his work to indicate that he was ever in need of money, or that the world weighed heavily. From fifteen to seventeen he had moved in a realm of cathedral splendor; of rich, rustling colors, bells, and unearthly treble voices blossoming in chapel glooms. It was a realm walled against the clamors of the world, where no one hungered and no one worked—in the workaday sense of the word. From seventeen to twenty-three he sojourned in Cambridge, for him a similar realm, but with occasional glimpses of the world beyond, peopled by men in splendid attire, men whose speech was the speech of state and power, poetry and scholarship. And just when he himself was beginning to have a grasp of scholarship and poetry, the forces of power and state snatched him up, offering undreamed of rewards.

But while Marlowe's troubles were always special ones, the central thread of the pattern of his life, which was the color of violent death, was now unwinding; for it was through his first protectors that he met the men in whose presence he was cut down six years later at the age of twenty-nine.

CHAPTER IV

London and Environs

I.

'AND tis a prety toy to be a Poet' was a thought to savor. For the last time on a July day in 1587 Marlowe looked about him. Past the turreted clusters of college buildings lay the Cambridge countryside, its hot, sloping meadows flower-fragrant, the smooth-flowing Cam mirroring trees and sky. Musing of the future he walked, feeling his elation give way to nostalgia, then turned back to make an end. In the chamber that had been his home for six years he doffed his gown, tucked it into a trunk, donned doublet and hose and feathered hat, examined the sword he would strap to his side upon setting forth, yanked it this way and that to limber up his arm, saw how the scabbard must hang for the blade to clear. (If he did not then strap on the sword, it was in any event soon afterward that he did, for he was shortly using it.)

His effects in order, he stepped quickly across the Old Court, past the confines of Corpus and the rambling buildings of the university. His destination was the stable of Thomas Hobson, carrier, whose horses were for hire for the trip to London. 'Hobson's choice' was already a part of the language because of his rule against hiring out horses save in their turn, the one that was most rested being the one to go. 'This or none,' Hobson would say. To students leaving for London, he added the advice that they would get there early enough if they did not ride too fast.[1]

At twenty-three it was a light-hearted thing to set out for London, and there wasn't a youth in any English shire who wouldn't have changed places with Marlowe gladly, were it only to be bound apprentice and journeying city-ward for a life of labor. But to be twenty-three, and a poet, and headed for London!

From Cambridge Marlowe came, jogging on the great northern road that led to Bishopsgate, and saw the outlying reaches of London Town, thin trickles of houses past the city's walls. Something of the country still lingered there, and streets paused on the threshold of fields. But within the wall it was otherwise; from its seven gates there unfolded a maze of streets that shut out the light of day and country airs—narrow and dirty and ill-smelling, but bustling with life, loud with people: 'in euery street, carts and Coaches make such a thundering as if the world ranne vpon wheeles: at euerie corner, men, women, and children meete in such shoales, that postes are sette vp of purpose to strengthen the houses, lest with iustling one another they should shoulder them downe. Besides, hammers are beating in one place, Tubs hooping in another, Pots clincking in a third, water-tankards running at tilt in a fourth: heere are Porters sweating vnder burdens, there Merchants-men bearing bags of money, Chapmen (as if they were at Leape-frog) skippe out of one shop

Elizabeth's London

into another: Tradesmen (as if they were dauncing Galli-
ards) are lusty at legges and neuer stand still!' [2] To a
country bumpkin it might have been disheartening, but
not so to one who saw his destiny there, who carried a collection of manuscripts that stamped him to himself, and
would have to anyone versed in such matters, as a poet of
considerable achievement and even greater promise; who
came, not as a stranger, cloaked in loneliness, but as one
sure of a welcome at certain great men's houses. Such was
the home of Thomas Walsingham in Scadbury, some
twelve miles from the metropolis. Thither will we post,
after the sights of London, to meet the kinsman of Elizabeth's Secretary, and with him one or two of his household who are to be remembered.

From east to west, including Westminster, the city
swirled for four miles, and from north to south, pouring
over the river into Southwark, two miles. East and west,
north and south, brimful of music Marlowe made his way,
looking about him as young men newcome to the city always have looked—reveling in its sights, stirred by its
pageantry and multitudinous clamor. He saw the famous
moated Tower, walled in like a little town. He saw London Bridge, covered over with tenements, loud with the
cries of hawkers, and at the southern or Surrey end a
cluster of traitors' heads on poles, a horrible sight, but
one which even idlers failed to notice. By the riverside he
heard the watermen's cries of 'Eastward ho!' and 'Westward ho!' as they ferried passengers across the busy
Thames, saw the stately palaces of nobles on the bank,
their stone stairs lapped by the water, and squat St. Paul's

minus its steeple bulging out of the skyline, and around it in every direction the spires of churches hemming the cathedral in—119 of them for a city of 100,000 people.

He saw the ghosts in stone of the great religious houses suppressed by Henry VIII. The Greyfriars by Newgate had become Christ's Hospital for children; the Priory of St. Bartholomew was now St. Bartholomew's Hospital; the Priory of Bermondsey lived on as St. Thomas's Hospital. Others were only ruins, and over their grounds and past their massive portals dusk or fog tiptoed quietly.

The government of the hurly-burly metropolis was vested in the Lord Mayor, who was chosen from one of the twelve companies or guilds; twenty-six aldermen of the wards, and two sheriffs, each of which had his own compter or prison, one in the Poultry, the other in Wood Street. Under them ranged the menials of the law—watchmen with their lanterns and bells, constables and serjeants, catchpoles and beadles, the butts of citizens' jokes, yet feared withal, and with good reason, for if they once clapped hand on shoulder it was difficult to wriggle free. Five prisons in the city proper—the Cage, Cripplegate, Fleet, Ludgate and Newgate—and five across the river in Southwark—the Clink, Compter, Marshalsea, King's Bench and White Lion—attested to this with their pent-up swarms. More sinister for the malefactor was the old saw: London juries hang half and save half.

Hanging was a spectacle, whether at Tyburn where thieves and murderers dangled a while and then were disemboweled with precise thrusts, or at Execution Dock, below Wapping Old Stairs, in Limehouse, where pirates

were trussed up at low tide and the water rose over them.
There was also Tower Hill, where the ax flashed swiftly
to the block. For the vagabond there were whipping posts,
for the beggar, stocks; and bawds and harlots might be
seen walking barebacked behind a cart, with a whipping
at the corners to bring derisive apprentices out of their
shops to gape.

Such was the London of the workaday world. At night,
lanterns jutting out at all angles from ivy-covered walls
in winding streets threw flickers of weird light as the wind
rose or fell and mist turned into fog. Overhead, the tall
houses met and conferred above the middle of the street,
and many of the streets were mostly in shadow—therefore
dangerous. Rogues trod the deeper darkness close to the
wall, their eyes peering wild for prey. After a good haul,
these sly ones, whose business was in the open, made for
the rendezvous of their giggling doxies; and priggers of
prancers and kinching coes, dummerers and jarkmen,
joined in uproarious tavern merriment with dells and
bawdy baskets, queans and other species of hussy.[3]

Taverns! It was a city full of them, and if the wind
but stirred, a legion of painted signs flapped and creaked
to heaven of good cheer below. From Whitehall to Charing Cross you might see the *White Hart*, the *Red Lion*,
the *Mermaid*, the *Three Tuns*, the *Salutation*, the *Grey-
hound*, the *Bell*, and the *Golden Lion*. In the very sight
of Charing Cross stood the *Garter*, the *Crown*, the *Bear
and Ragged Staff*, an *Angel* and a *King Harry Head*.
Thence, as you wandered toward the heart of the city, you
might pass another *White Hart*, the *Eagle and Child*, the

Helmet, the *Swan*, another *Bell*, another *King Harry Head*, the *Flower de Luce*, an *Angel* again, the *Holy Lamb*, the *Bear and Harrow*, the *Plough*, the *Ship*, the *Black Bell*, still another *King Harry Head*, a *Bull Head*, a *Golden Bull*, another *Flower de Luce*, a *Red Lion*, the *Horns*, *White Horse*, *Princess's Arms*, *Belle Savage's Inn*, *St. John the Baptist*, *Talbot*, *Ship of War*, *St. Dunstan*, *Hercules* (or the *Old Man Tavern*), a *Mitre*, again a *King Harry Head*, another *Three Tuns* and the *Three Cranes*—inns that called to you whatever your profession, that beckoned the soldier and sailor, the courtier stealing away from the court, the farmer on a visit from the country—in Thomas Heywood's rhymed catalogue:

> The Gentry to the *King's Head*,
> The Nobles to the *Crown*,
> The Knights unto the *Golden Fleece*,
> And to the *Plough*, the Clown.
> The Churchman to the *Mitre*,
> The Shepherd to the *Star*,
> The Gardener hies him to the *Rose*,
> To the *Drum* the man of war.

In Cheapside stood a more famous *Mitre* and a more famous *Mermaid*—that inn of wine and wit that was to be memorialized by Beaumont. There was a third *Mitre* in Fleet Street, a thoroughfare of side shows and wonders from abroad where the gullible parted from their pence to stand and gape. In Eastcheap flapped the sign of the *Boar's Head* over one of the chief inns of London. Mark, also, the *Sign of the Bishop* at Gray's Inn Lane's End, in Holborn.

But most of all a young writer might love St. Paul's, within whose yard and against whose weather-beaten sides nestled the shops of stationers and booksellers, with signs of their own to mark their establishments—'in Paules Churchyeard, at the Signe of the Blacke Beare,' or 'neere the little North doore of Saint Paules Church at the Signe of the Gun' the title-pages said. There, anticipation of his new life fired his mind; he stood in the Cathedral's clang-orous purlieus resolving high exploits—confident, self-assertive, and with a rare talent to mark him from his fellows. Now it was:

> The sight of London to my exiled eyes,
> Is as Elizium to a new come soule,

but later, when he had probed it to the depths, he added a sullen line to this exclamation:

> Not that I loue the citie or the men.

Now, however, all was exultation, a will to succeed; freedom was like wine, and Cambridge a fast-fading dream of prison.

2.

North of the city, past Bishopsgate, lay the Liberties of Norton Folgate and Shoreditch, suburbs beyond the wall where the sheriffs of London durst not go. There, impecunious actors and authors dwelt side by side, and life was not oppressive with conventions.

From time out of mind plays had been performed in the yards of the larger inns—the *Cross Keys* in Gracechurch Street, the *Bull* in Bishopsgate Street, the *Belle Savage* on Ludgate Hill. But the city authorities, by their own Puritanical leanings and prompted by vociferous preachers, harried the players. The old, old cry against delight was morality—'the inordynate hauntynge of greate multitudes of people, speciallye youthe, to playes, enterludes and shewes' for pleasure, which endangered their salvation. In addition, the coming of plague brought edicts against large gatherings. A way out had to be found if the wandering companies of actors were to survive, and the times called forth the men.

The theater has always attracted persons remarkable for their eccentricities. Perhaps no more remarkable characters ever counted the attendance and computed their profits than the two men we are about to meet.

In 1574, James Burbage, a joiner or carpenter, together with four 'servants' of the Earl of Leicester, had obtained a royal warrant to perform 'comedies, tragedies, enterludes and stage playes' subject only to the censorship of the Master of the Revels and restrictions 'in time of common prayer' and 'great or common plague.' The protection of a powerful nobleman was thought a help, but the preachers had the last thundering word: 'the cause of plagues is sin, if you look to it well: and the cause of sin are plays: therefore the cause of plagues are plays.' As

a result, in 1576 Burbage left the city in quest of freedom and profit. In the Liberty of Shoreditch he found
what he wanted, cheap land close to the metropolis; and
there, within the precincts of the old, dissolved Holywell
Priory, he erected in partnership with his brother-in-law
the first permanent building for theatrical purposes in
England. It was an innyard without the inn, but circular
instead of rectangular. He called it *The Theatre*—there
was no other.

When the venture proved profitable, another theater
followed Burbage's close by. It was called the Curtain.

The troubles of Master Burbage were not over, for the
preachers went on thundering against plays and players,
and pestilence closed the playhouses. But The Theatre
flourished, and with it the family fortunes. Shoreditch was
close enough to the city for a host to come trooping out
when a performance was given, and the Curtain proved
to be an additional lure. His son, Richard, acted at The
Theatre and eventually became the star of Shakespeare's
plays.

Re-entering London through Bishopsgate, you went
down Bishopsgate Street, thence through Eastcheap, and
so to the river and London Bridge. Across the river in
Southwark, in the Liberty of the Clink, there lived one
Philip Henslowe, a man with a restless and acquisitive disposition, versatile at turning all things that came his way
to a profit. Even in marriage thought of aggrandizement
must have been uppermost, for he took for his wife the
well-to-do widow of his former employer. Nominally a

dyer—Shakespeare's 111th Sonnet may contain a reference to him—

> my nature is subdu'd
> To what it works in, like the dyer's hand—

Henslowe found time from his trade for a number of profitable ventures—management of a bear-baiting house, pawnbroking, rental of tenements, and collector of rents from brothels for the Bishop of Winchester, whose palace stood by the riverside; hence the term 'Winchester geese' for prostitutes, and Gloucester's salutation to the Bishop himself: 'Winchester goose!' in *Henry VI*.

Casting about for a further source of revenue, Henslowe hit upon the idea of building a theater in Southwark. As this involved a considerable expenditure, in 1587 he went into partnership with John Cholmley of London, grocer. Under the terms of the partnership, Cholmley agreed to pay Henslowe 816 pounds, in quarterly instalments of 25 pounds, 10 shillings, over a period of eight and a quarter years, receiving in return half the receipts and continued occupation of a small house near the property to be erected. Thus Henslowe secured for himself receipts of 102 pounds a year, for which insurance he was willing to forego half the profits of his theater for the length of the partnership. It was a shrewd piece of business, entirely in his favor while the profits of the joint venture were under 204 pounds a year, and when they were over that sum he received half the profits plus 102 pounds.

The building erected on this financial foundation was

the Rose theater.[4] One of the actors of Henslowe's acquaintance was Edward Alleyn, who became his son-in-law, his partner and the creator of Tamburlaine, Faustus, Barabas and other Marlovian roles; and the founder of Dulwich College—some say because of a vow when the devil appeared on the stage during a performance of *Dr. Faustus.*

3.

If you followed the looping Thames eastward from Southwark, past the Surrey end of London Bridge, you came to a little village called Deptford. There lay the *Golden Hind,* the first English ship to voyage around the world; on its deck, in 1581, Elizabeth had knighted its commander, Francis Drake. The ceremony was long since over, but the ship stayed, a floating inn, until time and souvenir hunters picked it to pieces. It was the show place of Deptford, itself so tiny a place that on pictorial maps of the time the steepled Church of St. Nicholas sufficed to represent it. There was a tavern there, too, but of this later.

Past Deptford, stemming from Thames' side, flowed the Ravensbourne river, and there were country roads, meadows and woods. When London was infested with plague, as it was like to be in the spring of the year, Deptford was a pleasant place to pass the time. We will return to it on a May day six years later; for the present mark, if you will, the church with its quiet fold of graves, the church and the tavern.

CHAPTER V

Glimpse of a Slayer

I.

A DOZEN miles from London, in a southeasterly direction, stood the village of Chislehurst with its church and steeple, the Reverend Richard Harvey, rector. Scadbury Manor was also in Harvey's parish, and there lived Thomas Walsingham and his wife Audrey.

We do not know when and how Thomas Walsingham and the poet met. We know that he 'bestowed many kind fauors' on Marlowe 'in his life time' (an inference of patronage which we get from the dedication of *Hero and Leander*); and that it was a member of his household who killed Marlowe. We also know that welcome at his table was a friend of Marlowe's—older, proud, and a master of the jest that thrusts like a rapier. He is Thomas Watson, Latinist and poet, a man full of flourishes, who cannot write a sonnet without prefixing a paragraph, like a poetical exegetist, placing a nosegay in prose above the flowers of his verse, so that the odor of his learning is twice-distilled; and he signs himself, on the title-pages of his Latin works, 'Thomas Watsonus, I.V., studiosus'— that is, student of either law, canon and civil, for he had studied both. He comes dressed in the finery of the Italianate Englishman (a favorite howl of the preachers);

but he is scholarly, learned, broadly read, a traveler and erst a sojourner on the Continent—in short, a man of the world, one who had spent his time at Oxford, like Marlowe at Cambridge, 'not in logic and philosophy, as he ought to have done; but in the smooth and pleasant studies of poetry and romance.' [1]

Watson's friendship with Thomas Walsingham was of long standing. It began in Paris, during Sir Francis Walsingham's tenure as ambassador.

Watson is also Marlowe's particular friend. Shortly their lives will be inextricably linked in Newgate *dossiers*. Marlowe survived their perilous relationship; the three men who follow cut his survival short.

2.

Deep in the politico-religious intrigue that brought Mary Stuart to the block and, as one of its manifestations, took Marlowe from Cambridge to Rheims 'in matters touching the benefitt of his Countrie' was one Robert Poley, Privy Council spy. So skillfully did Poley weave himself back and forth, ostensibly in the pay of Secretary Walsingham to spy on the Catholic conspirators, but taking his reward from two sources, that none can say where his allegiance lay. It was not for nothing that Poley said of himself: 'I will sweare and forsweare my selffe rather then I will accuse my selffe to doe me any harme.' It had been Thomas Walsingham's task to interrogate him as the Babington plot blazed forth brightly—and then the government struck, quenching the flame and snuffing out the lives of the plotters.

That Poley should have been welcome at Scadbury is perhaps not surprising in that age of conspiracy; and thither the spy and complotter went, to entreat further service or reward, and to continue his friendship with one who was employed there, Ingram Frizer, the Walsinghams' 'man,' privy to his master's and mistress's affairs, the agent and overseer of their household—a prototype of Elizabethan servant and rogue who, as Marlowe observed, to 'get you any fauour with great men'

> must be proud, bold, pleasant, resolute,
> And now and then, stab as occasion serues.

Among Frizer's recent purchases was a dagger of steel costing twelve pence.

Frizer had a hanger-on named Nicholas Skeres, described in a Middlesex *dossier* of 1585 as one of a number of 'maisterles men & cut-purses, whose practice is to robbe Gentlemen's chambers and Artificers' shoppes in & about London.'

Such men as these, besides poets, hovered about the house in Scadbury. We will meet this trio again—and with them Marlowe—in the tavern in Deptford in 1593.

CHAPTER VI

Marlowe and Shakespeare

I.

THE year 1587 was a time of marching men and far-flung stirrings against the order of things. The Duke of Parma's soldiery harried the Low Countries for an inquisitorial God. In Ireland, Elizabeth's Lord Deputy donned armor over his soul, burning and pillaging to bring an oppressed folk into submission; only the gallows had a yield where his soldiers passed. In Spain the Armada was building; the din of its multitudinous labors blew loud into England.

Who with these facts in view can doubt that that part of the poetic process which deals with the selection of subject matter is less of a mystery than scholars have supposed? To Marlowe, newcome to London to commence writing, fresh from his Privy Council mission and his triumph over the Cambridge dons, his mind full of images of ruthless powers at work and stored to the brim with the treasure of his reading, only the clanking march of men-at-arms, there or abroad, might be the catalyst. The rest is labor—long, arduous, but no mystery.

He unpacks his belongings, his dog-eared books emerge from trunk's depth, and he spreads fair paper on a table, places inkhorn and goose quill at hand, and bends over in his chair to chart his course, the mariner of his fate; but whether in Shoreditch, where stood the two playhouses, The Theatre and Curtain, or in the Liberty of Norton Folgate, adjacent to Shoreditch, where likewise good company was to be found, there is no way of telling, for he wasn't in trouble at this time, and there is therefore no trace of him. But while, for the present, his legal *dossier* remains without addition, he is himself writing his own chief record for after-men, his work.

Beginning at Corpus Christi, a succession of ponderous volumes had brought to maturity in his thoughts the conquering figure of Tamburlaine the Great—among them Pedro Mexia and the authors in his bibliography: 'This then that I here geue you, that al haue I borrowed of *Baptista Fulgotius*, Pope *Pius*, *Platina* vppon the life of *Boniface* the ninth, of *Mathew Palmier*, and of *Cambinus* a Florentine, writyng the historie, and exploytes of the Turkes;' Paulus Jovius, Petrus Perondinus—dead names of once living and learned men, one a bishop, one, even, a Pope.

The East blazed with glory in men's imaginations; their books and their table talk brought tidings little less opulent than the goods in their ships' holds. Now, before him on the table, in the fabulous maps of Ortelius, sprawl the continents of Asia and Africa—on these he has gazed until the music and magnificence of their place-names are steeped in his mind. Not for him the couplets of his contemporaries, the smooth song of seasons or of love, the lines ending on the inevitable chime or jingle—although here and there admirable of their kind and inspiring. In-

Tamburlaine

the Great.

Who, from a Scythian Shephearde,
by his rare and woonderfull Conquests,
became a most puissant and migh-
tye Monarque.

And (for his tyranny, and terrour in
Warre) was tearmed,
The Scourge of God.

Deuided into two Tragicall Dif-
courses, as they were sundrie times
shewed vpon Stages in the Citie
of London.

By the right honorable the Lord
Admyrall, his seruantes.

Now first, and newlie published.

LONDON.
Printed by Richard Ihones: at the signe
of the Rose and Crowne neere Hol-
borne Bridge. 1590.

stead, with contempt for the usual forms and the writers who observed them, he begins thus:

> *From iygging vaines of riming mother wits,*
> *And such conceits as clownage keepes in pay,*
> *Weele lead you to the stately tent of War,*
> *Where you shall heare the Scythian Tamburlaine*
> *Threatning the world with high astounding tearmes.*

Exultation rings the deep bell of his being. Like combers making toward the land, treading the offshore deeps with flashing, rhythmic thunder, the music of his marching iambics surges forward, thundering harmony to the shores of consciousness. Deftly, wasting few lines, for he has learned the lesson of plot and counterplot, he sketches the weak, wavering Mycetes, King of Persia, and his aggressive brother, Cosroe, whom the revolting nobles of the realm acclaim

> Emperour of *Asia,* and of *Persea,*
> Great Lord of *Medea* and *Armenia:*
> Duke of *Affrica* and *Albania,*
> *Mesopotamia* and of *Parthia,*
> East *India* and the late discouered Isles,
> Chiefe Lord of all the wide vast *Euxine* sea,
> And of the euer raging Caspian Lake.[1]

This is already, albeit in little, the aspiring protagonist of Marlowe's mind; but Tamburlaine dwarfs Cosroe (as all Marlowe's chief characters dwarf the casts they head):

His looks do menace heauen and dare the Gods.

And it is the beginning of the Marlovian beat that shortly will rise into such freedom and such music as the theater and poetry had never known, the melodic measure that is without equal in English blank verse:

> Your Maiestie shall shortly haue your wish,
> And ride in triumph through *Persepolis.*
>
> And ride in triumph through *Persepolis?*
> Is it not braue to be a King, *Techelles?*
> *Vsumcasane* and *Theridamas,*
> Is it not passing braue to be a King,
> And ride in triumph through *Persepolis?*

> O my Lord, tis sweet and full of pompe.

He has but begun to bring up, from the rich mines of his mind, the treasure heaped there; yet not all the kings in *Tamburlaine* speak with splendor, and one utters the thought of modern man:

> Accurst be he that first inuented war.

2.

This is the lost time of Marlowe's apprenticeship to the theater, and not too much may be hazarded. However—
There was present in London at this time a young man two months his junior who, like himself, had recently embarked on a career of his own in the theatrical quarters

of the metropolis. He was not a university man, and he
began more like a plodder than a poet, but he was versatile, able to write or correct a line, and speak it, too; and
therefore useful around a theater.

When Marlowe had finished his play, he put the manuscript under his arm and set out to get it produced. The
title-page of the first edition states that it was 'sundrie
times shewed vpon Stages in the Citie of London' 'By the
right honorable the Lord Admyrall, his seruantes.' As
the Admiral's men acted in the great innyards of the city
as well as at The Theater and Rose, there is now no way
of telling where Marlowe's opus was first presented. Was
it Burbage that he interviewed at the Theatre in Shoreditch, or was it Henslowe at the Rose in Southwark? Was
it in Shoreditch or Southwark that he met, one day, the
youth from Stratford, Will Shakespeare, and saw for the
first time the high, intellectual brow, the deep, calm eyes,
the sensitive nose and the mouth shaped to wisdom, of
him whom unborn generations were to know by portrait
and book? That they met, that they afterwards collaborated, is certain; the work that bears Shakespeare's name
and which is, in part, Marlowe's, testifies to this, as do the
fond remembrances of the surviving poet when the fiery
young man from Cambridge was dead.[2]

There was a contrast here—the one discreet, quiet-
spoken, seeking to please, and as yet known but to few—
the other, impulsive, reckless, the spendthrift of his
genius, already befriended by the great; one, looking with
grave eyes upon the world of men about him, already
noting and comprehending all, but nursing his great

powers against maturity—the other, pouring forth at the start his mind's riches, and accepting fame, when it came suddenly, as his due. Between such opposites—Shakespeare, the mature youth, and Marlowe—there could have been no envy. There is evidence of friendship.

Fame came suddenly to Marlowe, via *Tamburlaine*. The success scored by his play is attested, in the absence of other records, first, by the imitations that were rushed to the stage, and, second, by the numerous allusions to it in the writings of his contemporaries and successors.[3] Of the men from whom he had learned much, though taking little, Buckhurst still lived—in the service of the state, not the theater; Gascoigne was dead; and Peele evened the score—if score there was—by writing several plays in Marlovian rhythms—*Edward I, The Battle of Alcazar, David and Bethsabe*. Robert Greene, by this time one of the London luminaries, was outwardly contemptuous; nevertheless, he wrote *Alphonsus King of Aragon* in direct imitation of *Tamburlaine*, just as he was to write *Friar Bacon and Friar Bungay* in imitation of *Faustus*. Collaborating with Thomas Lodge in *A Looking Glasse for London and England*, Greene again fell under the sway of the newcomer he pretended to despise, and his fellow-writer with him.

3.

To a theater overhung with the pall of pedantry, Marlowe brought life and light; to men like Shakespeare, new impetus and inspiration. Writers writhing at his success might attack his 'high astounding tearms,' but London's audiences wanted more. They got it.

It was not only the immediate popularity of the First Part of *Tamburlaine* that made Marlowe eager to pen a sequel and the Admiral's men to present it:

> *The generall welcomes Tamburlain receiu'd,*
> *When he arriued last vpon our stage,*
> *Hath made our Poet pen his second part.*

The year 1587 marked the beginning of the critical phase in Elizabeth's relations with her erstwhile brother-in-law Philip. Then Drake's guns pounded the Spanish coast to stave off the peril of the Armada for another year, and once more the issue remained unresolved. It was like Europe before 1914—and 1939: tension and incidents. When war came, it came to many as a relief.

It came undeclared, but the nation was ready. Great stores of ammunition had been gathered, and the shires of England rang to the clatter of drilling yeomanry. The battlefields of the Low Countries had been for decades a Continental academy for her soldiers. The ships that were her floating defense had been refurbished and rearmed. It was Henry VIII who created England's naval power, and it was fitting that his daughter should prove it.

On July 19, 1588, watches on the shore beheld the floating city of the Invincible Armada, carack and galleon, galley and pinnace, walloping the water in a vast array, their myriad banners staining the Channel air, their sides studded with guns, their decks thickly clustered by knights and soldiers. When, after wind, water and fire, and the English valor, had beaten them off and scattered their remnants as far as the coast of Ireland, England's exultation blazed forth: bonfires in the streets, beacon fires on the hills, prayers in crowded churches, and the clangor of pealing church bells over all.[4]

Reader, reading the words of the preacher at Paul's Cross, August 20, at the first public service of thanksgiving, how did the fourth decade of the twentieth century differ for England and, indeed, the world?—'They communed of peace, and prepared for most cruel warre: for they thinke that no faith nor trueth is to be kept with vs, but that they may feine dissemble, breake promise, sweare, and forsweare, so they may deceiue vs, and take vs vnwares, and oppress vs sodainely.'

Then it was the Spaniard and salvation, latterly the German and a new doctrine. Then: 'The Lord arose, and took the cause (*which indeede was his owne*) into his owne hands, and fought against them, that fought against vs.'[5]

Of the multitude that heard these words, it is unlikely that Marlowe made one. It was not his wont to favor preachers with attention, and he had a task to do.

4.

Once more he has turned to his books; but now he can only glean where earlier he had reaped. The maps of Ortelius are still his guide to the Asia and Africa overrun by Tamburlaine's victorious armies; but an incident in the *Rervm Vngaricarvm Decades Qvattvor* of An-

tonius Bonfinius leads him to start his sequel in southeast-
ern Europe. It is not essential to the plot, but it appealed
to Marlowe for another reason.

The incident deals with the truce between the Turkish
potentate Amurath II and Vladislaus of Poland and Hungary, one of the kings of the Christian league. Their truce
permitted the infidel monarch to withdraw his troops from
Turkish Europe, he having murderous business elsewhere.
It was sworn to in the name of Christ and Mahomet, but
was nevertheless denounced by the papal legate, Cardinal
Julian, who urged the immediate invasion of Amurath's
undefended provinces: 'Against a perfidious enemy the
use of every art, power and stratagem is permissible; art is
eluded by art, stratagem is to be circumvented by stratagem,' were his words, and, calling the Christian kings to
holy war, he absolved them in the name of the Pope, with
the assurance that 'nothing will be more pleasing to Christ
all-good and all-powerful, or more honorable to your-
selves.' The lay mind can only react like Marlowe's
monarch:

> Can there be such deceit in Christians?

At Varna on the Black Sea, whither he marched in
wrath, the Turk met the perfidious Christians and de-
feated them—after calling on Christ to avenge the wrong
done to his name. The battle took place in 1444; Marlowe pushed back the date half a century to Tamburlaine's
time, making Sigismund of Hungary the Christian leader
who broke faith with the infidel, and Orcanes, King of

Natolia, his adversary—and these are the men as the issue
is decided:

Sig. Discomfited is all the Christian hoste,
And God hath thundered vengeance from on high,
For my accurst and hatefull periurie.

Orc. Now lie the Christians bathing in their bloods,
And Christ or *Mahomet* hath bene my friend.

But a fellow monarch blurts out (in Marlovian tones):

Tis but the fortune of the wars my Lord,
Whose power is often proou'd a myracle.

With this as prelude, Marlowe's anticlerical bias,
whetted at King's School, sharpened at Corpus Christi,
breaks forth in marshaled, derisive thrusts against religion
and its servitors—although not yet his countrymen's,
which had its advantages; and long before the coming of
the Nazis he saw the spectacular element in the burning
of books to make the foolish gape, letting Tamburlaine
dare Mahomet out of heaven to save his holy writ, which
the fire consumes. If some of his contemporaries began
early to call him an atheist, it could not have been unexpected, although he must have thought them dolts considering the other wares he had to offer.

5.

Let us glance a moment at some of his wares—there will be enough and to spare of the other thing before his story ends. In the Second Part of *Tamburlaine* they appear early and in profusion, and they remain so up to the close:

> The Grecian virgins shall attend on thee,
> Skilful in musicke and in amorous laies:
> As faire as was *Pigmalions* Iuory gyrle,
> Or louely *Io* metamorphosed.

There is an echo from Ovid here, but the pupil has left the house of his master; and an echo of lost orthodoxy:

> Now walk the angels on the walles of heauen,
> As Centinels to warne th' immortall soules,
> To entertaine deuine *Zenocrate*.

> The Cherubins and holy Seraphins
> That sing and play before the king of kings,
> Vse all their voices and their instruments
> To entertaine diuine *Zenocrate*.

At twenty-four we find him rehearsing the great scene of his greatest work, prefiguring at the conclusion of the long, lyric elegy of undying love delivered by Tamburlaine the appearance of Helen before Faustus:

Tamburlaine's Map:

Africa by Ortelius

Now are those Spheares where *Cupid* vsde to sit,
Wounding the world with woonder and with loue,
Sadly supplied with pale and ghastly death:
Whose darts do pierce the Center of my soule.
Her sacred beauty hath enchaunted heauen,
And had she liu'd before the siege of *Troy*,
Hellen, whose beauty sommond Greece to armes,
And drew a thousand ships to *Tenedos*,
Had not bene nam'd in *Homers* Iliads;

while in the conqueror's rage at the gods for the death
of his beloved there is an overtone of Marlowe's own de-
fiance, the play's final thunder and orchestration of:

Come let vs march against the powers of heauen,
And set blacke streamers in the firmament,
To signifie the slaughter of the Gods.[6]

To dying Tamburlaine 'one brings a Map'—Marlowe's
Ortelius—and the Scythian reviews the long line of his
victories, the resounding place-names tumbling like boul-
ders into the meadows of his marches. His farewell to his
sons and his chieftains is one long regret that he must leave
territories yet unconquered; and in the pause of the dying
fall of the versification we sense the intellectual Marlowe's awareness of the vast, unexplored world of his
time:

                                    the golden Mines,
Inestimable drugs and precious stones,
More worth than *Asia,* and the world beside,

And from th' Antartique Pole, Eastward behold
As much more land which neuer was descried.

The age he lived in was one of enterprise and adventure
with which his restless being was in tune. But Marlowe
was aware that strenuous living and fabulous pursuits, for
honor and for gold, were not all. The man who could
write:

Our soules, whose faculties can comprehend
The wondrous Architecture of the world:
And measure euery wandring plannets course,
Still climing after knowledge infinite,
And alwaies moouing as the restless Spheares,

stands close to our time. His work is full of the imagery
of a new day—of exploration and discovery in the realms
of knowledge as well as of colonization, of Bacon as well
as Raleigh. It is an imagery which he helped to shape,
and it sheds its light on the pages of the greatest Elizabethans, the light of 'unpath'd waters, undream'd
shores.' He came,

rich in fit epithets,
Blest in the louely marriage of pure words,

creating at the start of his career the prototype of a new
breed of stagemen, cruel and aspiring, but filled with immortal longings which are his own—all losers in the end,
but after what magnificent flights of power! The first is
Tamburlaine,

Of stature tall, and straightly fashioned,
Like his desire, lift vpwards and diuine,

who speaks with the speculative mind of his creator, voic-
ing for him, amid the shock of war, Marlowe's hymn to

Emperor As Footstool To Tamburlaine

beauty, a gathering harmony climaxed in the passage
which has been perhaps too much praised, that marvel-
ously melodic definition of beauty that fails to define or
to satisfy (except the puerile)—

If all the pens that euer poets held, *etc.*

He brought to the new-born theater the element that
quickened it into life—a youthful poetry of rhythms never
before seen in print or heard on the stage. It was profuse
and exuberant, and sometimes it spilled over into a stage
direction:

> *Alarums within, The Duke* Ioyeux *slaine.*
> *Enter the King of* Nauarre *and his traine;*

for his work is the work of one forever young and scornful
of the pedantic mind that studies a medium to perfection
but lacks poetry to light up its depths or sound music to
pierce the soul. It is a pageant of tall figures against a
silverfall of riches, the marriage of brightness with
brightness, music with music; and Marlowe unashamedly
exults and probes in the midst of puppets, however large
—for it is not the business of a young poet to be a de-
lineator of characters striding into life.

He is the true Elizabethan, voyaging on strange seas
to mine the mines of beauty. And he is lost to us, lost in
the corridors of the years, as one is lost who, turning his
back in a corridor of mirrors before we have seen his face,
is lost to sight, then reappears to stride silently in the
deeps of glass, an image that recedes, yet in a fixed moment is forever there, so that we seem to hear, along the
passageway, the fading footfall.

The face of this man is lost to us as a face is lost in the
crowd and jostle of a city street; another step, another
look, and the glimpse of strength or beauty may be ours—
splendor under the brim, the passionate glance; but we

cannot take that step, the look is not granted us; time takes the street from the striders in it, the minutes of time fall like rain on London streets, obliterating time and the dwellers in Elizabethan time; but in the cool depths of the past, his image glows as in a mirror; look now—it is the fixed moment: the passionate face where 'shin'd the quenchles fire' is there.

CHAPTER VII

First Salvos Against Marlowe

I.

IN HIS HOUSE in Shoreditch, another Cambridge Master of Arts heard the applause that rang in a new rival, and he stroked his red beard to a point, feeling the old soul-sickness of envy.

He is Robert Greene, a madcap fellow, with a fine strain of poetry in him, and a fine streak of malice. He is an established author—with a thin purse, to be sure; but never, until now, one to question his shortcomings. His books can fill a shelf, for he is an old hand at the writing game, and novels, pamphlets and poems have issued from his pen in profusion. In the theater, too, his score is a high one; but his reputation, for all that is unsavory: 'Who in London hath not heard of his dissolute, and licentious liuing; his fonde disguisinge of a Master of Arte with ruffianly haire, vnseemely apparell, and more vnseeme-lye Company'—'his continuall shifting of lodginges'—.

Thus runs, in part, the catalogue of his sins, chief of which is a shortage of money, and what killed him in the end, besides palpable disease, was a consumption of the purse. London meant good pickings for a time; uncertain, sporadic, the rack of morale; forced, frantic trips to pawn-brokers and play-brokers, or sweaty bargainings with the crabbed booksellers of St. Paul's; but times are changing, and he sees two young men at the van of a swarm invading those precincts where he has held sway, bearing under their arms new plots and manifestoes. The words of Marlowe's prologue rankle: 'From iygging vaines of riming mother wits . . . .' He has rather fancied his smooth couplets—who has not liked them? He reaches for his new manuscript—*Perimedes the Blacke-smith*—to insert a double blast loosed in the general direction of the upstarts' camp, lumping Marlowe and the other newcomer derisively together at the start, as he will do again in a final, bitter onslaught after life and hope have fled. His medium is the address 'To the gentlemen readers': 'I keepe my old course, to palter vp some thing in Prose, vsing mine old poesie still, *Omne tulit punctum*, although latelye two Gentlemen Poets, made two mad men of Rome beate it out of their paper bucklers: & had it in derision, for that I could not make my verses iet vpon the stage in tragicall buskins, euerie worde filling the mouth like the faburden of Bo-Bell, daring God out of heauen with that Atheist Tamburlan.'

He reads over each word with a hawk eye, satisfied they will set up a loud buzzing.

Of the first part of this mysterious palaver, what is to be made? One of the men he alludes to is undoubtedly Marlowe; is the other Shakespeare, and is the play he scoffs at, besides *Tamburlaine, The Tragedie of Titus Andronicus,* and did these two geniuses collaborate thus early in their careers, as they were to do later?

The mood wears off as Greene's miserable surroundings

come into focus again and the hag Poverty has him by the shoulder with a bony grip. But once more echoes of Marlowe's lines make distant thunder in his brain, and his fury, rigged out in scorn, stalks forth; 'but let me rather openly pocket vp the Asse at *Diogenes* hand: then wantonly set out such impious instances of intolerable poetrie: such mad and scoffing poets, that haue propheticall spirits as bred of *Merlins* race.' [1]

A tavern signboard and the Cambridge variant of Marlowe's name offer the opportunity for derision and a pun, to make Greene stroke his beard in satisfaction. It is an old trick in word-combat—*argumentum ad hominem*. His anger subsides, and he resumes patronizingly, mixing in a little mystery to soften the hard edges of his conceit: 'If there be anye in England that set the end of scollarisme in an English blanck verse, I thinke either it is the humor of a nouice that tickles them with self-loue, or to much frequenting the hot house (to vse the Germaine prouerbe) hath swet out all the greatest part of their wits, which wasts *Gradatim*, as the Italians say *Poco a poco*. If I speake darkely Gentlemen, and offend with this digression, I craue pardon, in that I but answere in print, what they haue offered on the Stage.'

He winds up ingenuously, if not with complete frankness—which is something. His reference to the sweat cure is ironic, however, for he died of syphilis. How bitter it must have been, after this attack, to find himself forced to imitate the novice's blank verse in order to get by at all! But that is what happened.

2.

These things he talks over with Thomas Nashe, another of the young men, but different, one who knows his place, which is that of disciple. Nashe, late a Bachelor of Arts of St. John's College, had known Marlowe at Cambridge, but zeal for the master makes him eloquent against his schoolmate. Perhaps their early familiarity helped—it nearly always does. For the present he lacks a vehicle in which to send his invective spluttering in print, for he is a genius at it. This lack is shortly supplied by Greene—'In a night & a day would he haue yarkt vp a Pamphlet as well as in seauen yeare, and glad was that Printer that might bee so blest to pay him deare for the very dregs of his wit'—as Nashe wrote later about his friend. Greene sees the advantage of another voice raised against Marlowe and, in addition, the proposal he makes Nashe is flattering, and gratitude in a disciple is good. He suggests that Tom write the preface to a new work of his entitled *Menaphon.* Even if it were the other way around, what a feather in Nashe's cap! He accepts eagerly, and the swagger in his walk enters his prose, for it is addressed 'To the Gentlemen Students of Both Universities': 'I am not ignorant how eloquent our gowned age is grown of late; so that euery mechanicall mate abhorreth the English he was borne to, and plucks, with a solemn periphrasis, his *vt vales* from the inke-horne: which I impute, not so much to the perfection of Arts, as to the seruile imitation of vaine glorious Tragedians, who contend not so seriously to excell in action, as to embowell the cloudes in a speech of comparison, thinking themselues more than initiated in Poets immortality, if they but once get *Boreas* by the beard and the heauenly Bull by the deawlap.

'But heerin I cannot so fully bequeath them to folly, as their ideot Art-masters, that intrude themselues to our eares as the Alcumists of eloquence, who (mounted on the stage of arrogance) thinke to out-braue better pennes with the swelling bumbast of bragging blanke verse.'

It is not yet the style of the swashbuckler in prose whose tracts discomfited and pursued Gabriel Harvey, the lover of books and hounder (as we shall see) of men who wrote them; it smacks still of Robert Greene, and indeed so much is the master in the mind of the disciple, that the thrust is as much for the friend as against the foe. He will do better than this in time; like the philosopher in Rabelais, he will thwack, bump, batter, knock, thrust, push, jerk, shock and shake his opponent when the grudge is great, but Marlowe is not his nemesis, and he is merely taking up the cudgels in behalf of another.

In any case, the foregoing did not prevent Nashe and Marlowe from becoming—or remaining—friends, and Nashe could write a few years later, and believe it to be the truth: 'I neuer abusd *Marloe.*'

3.

Like Greene, Tom Nashe was not content to direct his fire at a single foe. The salute to his friend and the shot at 'Art-master' Marlowe contains a sneering allusion to another of the London luminaries, Thomas Kyd, author of *The Spanish Tragedie* and a play about Hamlet.

Kyd was not one of the University wits. The son of a scrivener, or professional penman, his studies had been limited to the Merchant Taylors' school in East Smithfield, which the poet Edmund Spenser had also attended; Spenser, however, proceeded to Cambridge. There is no record to show that Kyd went any higher. It is possible that he supported himself for a time in his father's profession, for he could write both the Italian and English scripts.

The publication (in 1581) of *Seneca his tenne Tragedies translated into English* had a profound influence on Kyd. This is Nashe's commentary: 'It is a common practise now a dayes amongst a sort of shifting companions, that runne through euery Art and thriue by none, to leaue the trade of *Nouerint*, whereto they were borne, and busie themselues with the indeuors of Art, that could scarcely Latinize their neck verse if they should haue neede; yet English *Seneca* read by Candle-light yeelds many good sentences, as *Blood is a beggar,* and so forth; and if you intreate him faire in a frostie morning, hee will affoord you whole *Hamlets,* I should say handfuls of Tragicall speeches . . .'

That Kyd is surely meant is seen by the reference to *Nouerint,* from the phrase *Nouerint uniuersi per praesentes* [a] with which scriveners began their documents. As for his not being able to save himself from hanging by reading a Latin verse from the Bible, a quaint custom of

[a] Know all men by these presents.

the time, the man was too circumspect in his behavior to be in peril. It was only after he met Marlowe that trouble came—and then scholarship or the lack of it made no difference, although Nashe seems to think otherwise: 'what can be hoped of those that thrust *Elisium* into hell, and haue not learned, as long as they haue liued in the spheares, the iust measure of the Horizon without an hexameter. Sufficeth them to bodge vp a blanke verse with ifs and ands.'

In Act I of *The Spanish Tragedie,* Elysium is represented as being in the nether world, while in Act II occurs the line: 'What, Villaine, ifs and ands?'

Such things fluster a scholar.

4.

If Kyd counter-attacked, there is no record of it. But in Gabriel Harvey's brother Richard he found an unexpected challenger of Nashe's pretensions.

In the parish of the Thomas Walsinghams, the Reverend Richard Harvey, having digested Nashe's tract, and perhaps recalling something of the man from school days, set about taking him down a peg or two. He had come a long way from Saffron Walden via Cambridge divinity; and full of pious zeal, and with the example of his brother to spur him on, he is writing a book: *A Theologicall Discovrse of the Lamb of God and His Enemies: Contayning a briefe Commentarie of Christian faith and felicitie, together with a detection of old and new Barbarisme, now commonly called Martinisme.* Long book titles ran in the family.

It is the time of the Martin Marprelate controversy, when a reverend gentleman with literary ambitions might be supposed to have his hands full defending the established order, if he needs must write. But the Harveys were ever versatile, and Richard has a style: 'I was loth to enter this discourse, but vppon request where I might be commaunded: I prouoke not any but *Martin* who prouoketh all men: I was desired to giue like iudgement of certaine other, but it becummeth me not to play that part in Diuinitie, that one *Thomas Nash* hath lately done in humanitie, who taketh vppon him in ciuill learning, as *Martin* doth in religion, peremptorily censuring his betters at pleasure, Poets, Orators, Polihistors, Lawyers, and whome not? and making as much and as little of euery man as himselfe listeth. Many a man talketh of *Robin Hood,* that neuer shot in his bowe.'

This stung when it came Nashe's way, and in hot anger he wrote down: 'This is that *Dick* of whom *Kit Marloe* was wont to say that he was an asse, good for nothing but to preach of the Iron Age.'[2]

It sounds authoritative.

CHAPTER VIII

Preview of a Play

I.

I N THE SUMMER of 1589, Christopher Marlowe
and his friend Thomas Watson were both lodging in
the Liberty of Norton Folgate, north of the city, conveniently adjacent to Shoreditch where stood The Theatre
and Curtain. We know this, because trouble is at hand for
both.

Westward from Norton Folgate there extended a street
called Hog Lane which thrust through meadows to a
cluster of windmills in Finsbury Fields. Here, Marlowe
had observed, he could take the air in contemplative mood.

By night the taverns might draw him cityward, but St.
Paul's was the magnet by day. Swift trips down Bishopsgate Street, swinging past Cornhill and Cheapside, bring
him to the cathedral's stalls, to rummage for volumes for
his little library—new matter from the press to con, new
matter which, like the alchemist he is, he will transmute
into gold.

One day he found a prize.

2.

He is standing in Edward White's stall at the *Sign of
the Gun* near the north door of the Cathedral, his lip

curled in derision at the heaps of fatuous matter intended
for gulls, when he finds himself holding a paper-covered
pamphlet of some eighty pages, a translation with an
undistinguished format and a didactic title: 'THE HIS-
TORIE of the damnable life, and deserued death of *Doctor Iohn Faustus.*' [1]

What was there in this to charge his blood with elation,
so that his fingers tingled? Quickly he flipped over the
title-page, and saw there, at the top of the next page, the
argument of the book advanced: 'A Discourse of the most
famous Doctor Iohn Faustus of Wittenberg in Germanie,
Coniurer, and Necromancer: wherein is declared many
strange things that he himselfe hath seene, and done in
the earth and in the Ayre, with his bringing vp, his
trauailes, studies, and last end.' Once more he flips over
the page; and finds himself reading about a divinity student—about himself: 'Iohn Faustus, borne in the town of
Rhode, lying in the Prouince of *Weimer* in *Germanie*
. . . his father a poore Husbandman . . . but hauing an
Uncle at *Wittenberg* a rich man, & without issue, who
took this *I. Faustus* from his father, & made him his
heire, in so much that his father was no more troubled
with him, for he remained with his Uncle at *Wittenberg,*
where he was kept at ye Uniuersitie in the same citie to
study diuinity. . . .'

3.

To all men there come moments of exaltation because
chance is magically on their side, moments that are wholly

theirs because the luck that has befallen them was un-looked for yet was not altogether unexpected. Such moments are Marlowe's now, and a spell is over him as he reads on: 'But *Faustus* being of a naughty minde & otherwise addicted, applied not to his studies, but tooke himselfe to other exercises . . .' And still the parallel: '*Faustus* continued at study in the Uniuersity, & was by the Rectors and sixteene Masters afterwards examined how he had profited in his studies; and being found by them, that none for his time were able to argue with him in Diuinity, or for the excellency of his wisedome to compare with him, with one consent they made him Doctor of Diuinitie. But Doctor Faustus within short time after hee had obtained his degree, fell into such fantasies and deepe cogitations, that he was marked of many, and of the most part of the Students was called the Speculator. . . .'

4.

Quickly Marlowe thumbs through the chapter headings—'How Doctor Faustus began to practice in his diuelish Arte, and how he coniured the Diuel' . . . . 'The conference of Doctor Faustus with the Spirit Mephostophiles. . . .' The delectable headings are many. He calls for the bookseller, who comes apace, fingering his change. The purchase is made, and Marlowe hastens to his lodgings. He reads. He dreams. He writes.

Now comes Thomas Watson, to hear the gathering

symphony of his young friend's masterpiece and start the applause that is soon to ring out over London.

Poetry, however—his own or Marlowe's—is not the only concern of Watson at this time.

CHAPTER IX

Background of a Feud[1]

I.

THE *Sign of the Bishop* at Gray's Inn Lane's End creaked over one of the oldest inns in Holborn. It was a hospitable outpost for the traveler riding into London from Oxford or the west. The innkeeper was William Bradley, father of two sons, one named for him, who had not inherited his hospitable nature. The story of William Bradley the younger and his brother Richard indicates just the opposite.

The two brothers appear in the records as brawlers early in life. In 1582, when William was only nineteen, he and Richard got into a scuffle with one Zachary Sherme, a jerkin-maker's apprentice, who thwacked them both soundly. Thereupon the brothers ran howling to the law, and Zachary and his master were haled before Justice Robert Harrys, in Chancery, to present their recognizances 'for woundinge Richard and w^m the sonnes of w^m Bradley of Greys Inne lan inholder.' Bail was set at twenty pounds apiece, which gives the scuffle a rather serious sound. (In law, a recognizance is a bond or obligation, entered into and recorded before a court or magistrate, by which a person engages himself to perform some act or observe some condition, as to appear when called on,

86

to pay a debt, or to keep the peace; also, a sum of money pledged as a surety for such performance, and rendered forfeit by neglect of it.)

Four years later, in 1586, Mine Host Bradley himself appeared before Justice Harrys; but the record indicates that he stepped into a brawl in which Richard was a principal. In that year two sureties (or bondsmen) bound themselves in five pounds each in his behalf, and he himself for ten pounds, to keep the peace against two of his neighbors of Gray's Inn Lane, Thomas Oliver and John Norton. In filling out the form the court clerk put Richard's name down first, perhaps through familiarity, then substituted the father's—'pro [Richo] Willo Bradley de Greys Inn lane predicta Inholder.'

2.

The above may suffice for the Bradley family's background, at least as regards temperament. Master William Bradley's feud with Thomas Watson, gentleman and poet, would appear to be outside the scope of a mere brawler, but the few clues that have come down to us concerning their quarrel indicate there was nothing unusual about it, except for the turn it took. These clues are now presented in chronological order.

On March 8, 1588, young William bound himself to pay fourteen pounds on the following August 25 to John Alleyn of London, innholder and brother of Edward Alleyn, the actor. The money was never paid, for the bond remained in Alleyn's hands.

Alleyn's attorney was one Hugh Swift, who happened to be Watson's brother-in-law. Swift, it would appear, called on Bradley and threatened suit in the Court of Common Pleas if the money was not forthcoming. Bradley still demurred, and the issue remained in the air.

Bradley had for friend and neighbor, on the other side of Gray's Inn Lane opposite the *Bishop*, one George Orrell, a hard-bitten youth of his own age who lived to become a famous soldier in the Irish campaigns. Orrell is described as a man 'who holds his neck awry,' which may have been due to a natural defect; it may also have been brought about by a belligerent stance. Orrell, hearing the tale of his friend, sympathized, and offered his services in case of need. And so the matter dragged along through 1588.

Going to interview Bradley again in the summer of 1589, Swift was threatened with bodily harm by Orrell; whereupon the attorney sped before a justice. In the Queen's Bench Controlment Rolls, it is written: 'Hugo Swyfte petitions securities of the peace against George Orrell being in fear of death, etc.'

The petition was returnable November 25, during Michaelmas term.

3.

When Watson heard what had befallen his brother-in-law, he set forth in his company to corner Bradley, and with them went Alleyn, for it was his money that was involved. This sortie is evident from the next record, likewise garnered from the Queen's Bench Controlment Rolls: 'William Bradley petitions securities of the peace against Hugo Swyft & John Allen & Thomas Watson being in fear of death, etc.' With the petition went an attachment which directed the sheriff of Middlesex to order the three men to appear at Westminster Hall on November 25, but Bradley did not live to press his complaint.

The petitions of Swift and Bradley came so close together that both are recorded on the same membrane of parchment. Of the three men against whom Bradley petitioned securities of the peace, Watson with his elegant dress and Continental airs would have been the one to annoy the innkeeper's son most. In any case, it was Watson that he singled out for personal combat. On September 18 he walked the length of the city from Gray's Inn Lane to the Liberty of Norton Folgate in vengeful mood. Not finding Watson present, he strolled back and forth, nursing his wrath, in Hog Lane.

An hour or so later he was dead.

CHAPTER X

The Duel In Hog Lane

I.

THE troubles of his friend Watson, Watson's brother-in-law, *et al,* did not weigh heavily on the youthful shoulders of Christopher Marlowe. It would be his notion —having heard the tale—that if he met up with Master Bradley one of these days, he would give him a thrashing. But if a thrashing was out of the question—it was a grown man and a quarrelsome one, to boot—what then? Would it all end up in defiant words only, loud and derisive, like a pair of street hawkers? A pox on argument, thought Marlowe; he had a better tongue in his scabbard, one which words might not parry.

And so it fell out.

The scene is Hog Lane, Finsbury Fields. A patch of sky has fallen into the ditch at one end. In the background, three windmills flail the air, and sunlight catches the sail and flash of ponderous arms.

It is September 18, 1589, 'between the second and third hours after noon.' Two young men come face to face, and fall to with their swords. They are Christopher Marlowe and William Bradley. If they did anything more than confront each other and flash steel, the records are silent.

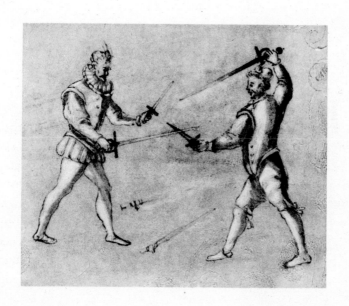

'Have At Ye'

As they lunged and thrust at each other, their mutterings and imprecations, and the clang of sword on sword, drew a crowd. None durst intervene, but all set up a clamor and craned necks for the constable. He was long in coming.

Up and down Hog Lane the brunt of battle bore them, and with them the lookers-on, a babble of voices and a swirl of legs. The two sworders, breathing heavily in their dance-of-death shuttle, grew arm-weary and faint.

In the background, the windmills flailed the air with rhythmic arms, looming like ogres as the eyes of the duellers caught the sail and flash of ponderous movement.

The next to come upon the scene was Thomas Watson, sword drawn. Hurling himself into the fray with suddenness, he took up the quarrel. Marlowe fell back, and Bradley assailed his new opponent:

'Art thou now come?' he said. 'Then I will have a bout with thee.'

He got more than he asked for, however. With sword and dagger he belabored Watson, but he had overreached himself in taking on a second comer. Watson, pressed hard, retreated before his sullen foe, but arriving shortly at the ditch at the end of Hog Lane, he stood his ground, his sword dissecting the threatening angles made by his opponent's sword and dagger. The longed-for opening suddenly came, and he thrust hard, driving the steel six inches into Bradley's chest. Sword and dagger clattered from Bradley's hands, and he sank, gushing blood, at Watson's feet. The crowd surged forward and closed in;

someone at the outer fringe ran pell-mell down Hog Lane, crying the news.

Into this hubbub of voices came the constable of Norton Folgate, Stephen Wyld. He needs no accusing finger to point out his man. Watson, disheveled, sword under arm, stands there, his face white and drawn. By his side is Marlowe, cheering his bruised friend.

The sequel is not long in coming. The two men, submissive to the law, are marched off to the nearest justice, Sir Owen Hopton, Lieutenant of the Tower of London. It was not to be the last time Marlowe would stand before him.

Dully the two men listen to the constable's harangue. A warrant is drawn up committing them to jail, and they are led across the city to Newgate.

This was the enrollment and the charge: 'Thomas Watson lately of Norton ffowlgate in Middlesex County, gentleman, & Christopher Marlowe lately of the Same, yoman, who were brought to the Gaole the xviij[th] day of September by Stephen wyld, Constable, both on Suspicion of Murder.' [1]

Before they are thrust into the prison's gloomy fastness, Marlowe sends word of his plight to one outside.

2.

The next day, Ion Chalkhill, gentleman, coroner of Middlesex County, summoned a jury of twelve worthy and law-abiding men, and the inquest got under way, 'in sight of the Body of William Bradley there lying dead and slain.' Marlowe and Watson appear, and they tell their story of self-defense with persuasive earnestness. Bradley is dead, and there are no interruptions. No death-bed statement is suddenly exhibited to confound the narrators. Watson's sword had done its work well, and the ghost of Hog Lane hovered mutely, if at all.

Now Master Chalkhill polls his jurors—'Geoffrey Witworth, william vernon, William Yomans, Peter Pawson, Thomas Cowper, John Holmes, Thomas Kingeston, John Harlowe, Richard Owen, william white, william Homan and John Hyde, worthy and law-abiding men of said Middlesex County, Who say upon their oath that, Whereas the aforesaid William Bradley and a certain Christopher Morley lately of London, gentleman, were on the xviijth day of September in the thirty-first Year above mentioned (i.e., of the Reign of Elizabeth) fighting together in a certain alley called hoglane in the parish of St. Giles without Creplegate in the aforesaid Middlesex County between the second and third hours after noon of that day: Thereupon, upon the clamor of the bystanders, in the same day and year and between the hours aforesaid, there did intervene a certain Thomas watson lately of London, gentleman, to separate the aforesaid William Bradley and Christopher Morley thus fighting and to preserve the said Queen's peace. And for that reason he then and there drew his sword. Whereupon the aforesaid Christopher Morley drew back & ceased to fight.'

It is like the clash between Tybalt and Mercutio in *Romeo and Juliet*—save that Marlowe is unscratched: 'And thereupon the aforesaid William Bradley, seeing the same Thomas watson thus intervening there with his sword drawn, spoke to him in the following English words, that is to say (*art thowe nowe come then I will haue a boute wth thee*). And instantly this william Bradley then and there made an assault upon the aforesaid Thomas watson and then and there wounded, struck and ill-treated the said Thomas watson with a sword and dagger of iron and steel, So that he despaired of his life. By reason of which the said Thomas watson with his aforesaid sword of iron and steel of a value of iii shillings iiij pence, which he then and there had and held in his right hand, did defend himself against the aforesaid William Bradley and fled from the aforesaid William Bradley for the saving of his life as far as to a certain ditch in the aforesaid alley, beyond which ditch this Thomas watson could not flee without peril of his life. And the aforesaid william Bradley continuing his aforesaid attack, had then and there closely followed the said Thomas Watson. Upon which the aforesaid Thomas Watson for the saving of his life then and there struck the aforesaid William Bradley with his sword aforesaid, giving him a mortal blow or wound in and upon the right side of the chest of the said william Bradley near the breast, six inches in depth and one in breadth, from which same mortal wound this William Bradley at ffynsebury in Middlesex County aforesaid instantly died. And so the aforesaid Jurors say upon their aforesaid oath that the aforesaid Thomas Watson killed and slew the aforesaid William Bradley in self-defense and in the manner and form aforesaid, against the said Queen's peace, crown and dignity, and not by felony nor

in any other way than is said above. In witness whereof
both the coroner and the Jurors have set their seals alter-
nately upon this Inquest.' [2]

It is all in legal Latin, save the taunt—'art thowe nowe
come'—by Bradley when Watson hove in sight. Master
Chalkhill has drawn up his document as the law required,
and his jurors concur in the finding, 'self-defense, in the
manner and form aforesaid'—all of them worthy and law-
abiding men—to Marlowe and Watson, snatched from
under the hangman's crossbar, most estimable, most
worthy, men of good sense all, from the foreman, Witworth, down to the last one. Leaving Finsbury, scene of
the inquest, they are led back to Newgate, secretly exulting. It was now only a matter of days or weeks—or
months, even, but what of that?—when due process of law
would set them free.

Time, however, was no longer a matter of expectant
reckoning to William Bradley, lying dead in Finsbury. A
sworder's thrust had put a red period to his twenty-six
years. There remained only to complete the record, in the
register books at St. Andrew's, that had been begun in
1562, when 'William Bradley sone of william Bradley
was Christined the xxviij of october.' And so, on September 19, 1589, an erstwhile likely lad, but quarrelsome,
was borne back to the parish of his birth, and there buried.

3.

Following the coroner's verdict, Marlowe was entitled
to bail. He needed only two men of substance who would

give their bond for his appearance at the next Gaol Delivery Sessions of Newgate, to be set free. He had sent word—would they come?

The answer is to be found in the Gaol Delivery Rolls: 'Middlesex. Be it remembered that, the first day of October in the year of the reign of our lady Elizabeth, Queen, etc., the Thirty-first, Richard Kytchine of Clifford's Inne, gentleman, & Humfrey Rowland of East Smithfeilde in the county aforesaid, horner, came before me, William Fletewoode, Sergeant at Law and Recorder of the City of London, one of the Justices of our lady the Queen appointed in the county aforesaid, & became sureties for Christopher Marley of London, gentleman: to wit, each of the sureties aforesaid under penalty of twenty pounds, and he, the said Christopher Marley, undertook for himself, under penalty of forty pounds of his and their and either of their goods, chattels, lands and tenements, to be levied to the use and behoof of our said lady the Queen on condition that he the said Christopher shall personally appear at the next Sessions of Newgate to answer everything that may be alleged against him on the part of the Queen, and shall not depart without the permission of the Court.' [3]

It is a recognizance binding Marlowe to appear at the Old Bailey on December 3, when 'the next Sessions of Newgate' were to be held. Eighty pounds was a lot of money to become liable for, but two weeks after the duel in Hog Lane, Richard Kitchen, attorney, and Humphrey Rowland, maker of horn handles and lantern windows, stood with the poet before Recorder Fleetwood and gave their word and their bond to set him free. All honor to them, although—money being what it is—they did it for a fee.

Watson, meanwhile, languished in Newgate. He was there eleven weeks, gnawing his impatience in its dark, damp, rat-infested depths. On December 3, he was led out into the daylight and, pale and blinking, brought into the Hall of Justice in the Old Bailey. Perhaps Marlowe saw his friend brought in, for he was there to fulfill the terms of his bond.

Now Watson stands before the bar. His head is up, his figure is tense. Before him sit the justices in their robes, an imposing array. A clerk intones: 'Thomas Watson, lately of London, gentleman, taken for cause shown in a certain Inquest taken in duplicate at ffynnesburie in Middlesex County the xxixth day of September in the xxxist Year of the Reign of Elizabeth, by god's grace Queen of England, ffrance and ireland, defender of the faith, &c., before Ion Chalkhill, gentleman, one of the Coroners of said Middlesex County, in sight of the Body of William Bradley there lying dead and slain.'

The inquest is handed up. The clerk who transcribes it is agitated, or his eyesight is bad, and he reads *xviij* as *xxviij;* getting into the thick of the fight in Hog Lane, he writes faster than his wont and gives Marlowe the name of William. At last it is over: 'Which Inquest of the said Coroner is now here recorded. And now cometh the aforesaid Thomas Watson before the aforesaid Justices, brought to the bar in his own proper person by the sheriff of the County aforesaid. And the Inquest aforesaid having been seen, the said Thomas Watson is remanded to prison by the Justices aforesaid in the custody of the said sheriff to await the Queen's grace.'

Now it is Marlowe's turn. In the margin of his recognizance, drawn up by Recorder Fleetwood who is now sitting as one of the justices at the Old Bailey, the clerk wrote: 'reu & del' per proclam'—'he returned and was quit by proclamation,' which relieved Master Kitchen and Master Rowland considerably. Shortly after, over in Newgate, in the margin of the parchment recording the imprisonment of the two poets, there was added before Watson's name, in Latin, the word 'bailed,' and before Marlowe's 'quit by proclamation.' Their troubles were now over, although Watson had to await the Queen's grace, or pardon, until February 10, 1590, two months and a week after his hearing at the Old Bailey. On that day, Queen Elizabeth at Westminster signed a bill of pardon which, like the Gaol Delivery document, rehearsed the coroner's inquest word for word, and concluded: 'We, moved with pity, have pardoned the said Thomas Watson the breach of our peace which concerns us against him for the aforesaid death. And we by these presents do give and concede to him our firm peace therefor. Upon the condition, however, that he will stand forth in our Courts should anyone desire to talk with him concerning the aforesaid death.' [4]

4.

Such were the coils a killer had to shuffle off to escape the hangman—but Marlowe was no sooner clear of the law than he put himself in mortal jeopardy again by a species of braggadoccio which seems incredible; he boasted 'That he had as good Right to Coine as the Queen of England, and that he was acquainted with one Poole a prisoner in Newgate who hath greate Skill in mixture of mettals and hauing learned some thinges of him he ment through help of a Cunninge stamp maker to Coin ffrench Crownes pistoletes and English shillinges'! The penalty for counterfeiting was boiling in oil.

There was something of the revolutionary in Marlowe; his rebellion against spiritual and temporal authority (and his innovations in the theater) show that; but it is difficult to believe that he was serious when he asserted that 'he had as good Right to Coine as the Queen' (even if he had no intention of exercising his 'right' equally with the sovereign by actually coining). There was also something childish in him; for if this utterance of his was merely a jest, and part of the tale of his sojourn in Newgate, it was unwise and dangerous to make it.

More easily understandable is the effect of his Newgate experience on his life and work. Waiting patiently for his sureties to come forward, waiting with growing anxiety for his release and the free air of London, waiting for the Queen's grace for Watson, how often must he have rehearsed the events of the duel and its aftermath in his mind—seen Bradley striding towards him in Hog Lane and the affray start which only death could terminate— seen Watson taking up the fight that he had begun—and the dead youth at their feet, dead, perhaps, because he, Marlowe, had not had the presence of mind to talk him out of his vengeful quest, and feeling the guilt of a co-murderer. In the Second Part of *Tamburlaine* occur the following lines:

> I know sir, what it is to kil a man,
> It works remorse of conscience in me.

CHAPTER XI

Raleigh, Spenser and Marlowe

I.

IT WOULD BE to your peril to glance at Sir Walter Raleigh as you might at a dapper jack or dandy, with contempt; but there he is, laced and jeweled, feathered and caped, the eyes hard that had seen America, but able to melt to softness over a girl in a garden [1] or steel themselves harder at the slaughter of a garrison; [2] limbs like ironwood under soft sleeves, and sword at side poised like a runner about to leap.

I see him treading the deck as the wind blows westward, crowding the sails of his ship on the Irish Sea—England aft, and with it the fading images of bustling streets, the whispering court already fawning on Essex, the new favorite. It was a shrewd move to absent himself—'he knew there was some ill office done him, that he durst not attempt to mind any other wayes, than by going aside; thereby to teach envy a new way of forgetfulnesse;' [3] strive with courtiers he would not, and perchance the Queen might question whither he had gone, for she was a woman, and had looked kindly on him.

He had come before her first during the Irish troubles, when his own colors flew in the field in the service of Lord Grey of Wilton, Spenser's master; but Raleigh was not one to abide the presence of a superior, and they fell out. The dispute that developed between Grey and Raleigh, says Naunton, 'drew them both over the Councell Table, there to plead their cause, where (what advantage he had in the cause, I know not) but he had much better in the telling of his tale; and so much, that the Queen and the Lords took no slight mark of the man, and his parts; for from thence he came to be known, and to have accesse to the Queen, and the Lords.'

When, for his services and his charm he was awarded estates in Munster and made Lord Warden of the Stanneries and Lieutenant of Cornwall by the queen's grace (for she never handed over cash when the means of making money would serve), their Lordships took fright at his rise: 'He had gotten the Queens eare at a trice, and she began to be taken with his elocution, and loved to hear his reasons to her demands: and the truth is, she took him for a kind of Oracle, which netled them all; yea, those that he relyed on, began to take his suddain favour as an Allarum, and to be sensible of their own supplantation, and to project his, which made him shortly after sing, *Fortune my foe.*'

Serving with Grey, he had become acquainted with his lordship's secretary, Edmund Spenser; pleasant recollections of the man and his work drew Raleigh to him now— this visit, and inspection of his Irish holdings, would suffice to occupy him until he deemed the time propitious for his return to England. It was thus that Spenser, dwelling at Kilcolman, in the county of Cork, received one day the soldier-poet he had never forgotten.

The visit marked a turning point in both their lives. A succession of unspectacular but steady posts in Ireland under the Crown had left Spenser, still a bachelor at thirty-seven, grooved in quietness, but writing voluminously; he had been granted the manor and castle of Kilcolman for his services, and was content, or so he deemed, with his lot. Talk of Irish affairs and the Armada, in the pursuit of which Raleigh had played a part, might fail to rouse his spirit to the point of adventure, but it must have been otherwise when his welcome guest chose literary London for his theme, bringing word of new writers, new plays. It was then that Spenser ventured to bring out the manuscript of *The Faerie Queene* to show his friend; and Raleigh found himself holding in his hands not only a jewel of rare price, but the opportunity to return to his royal mistress in triumph—sooner than he expected. His commendatory verse on Spenser's great poem leaves little doubt that it was he who urged the dedication of *The Faerie Queene* to 'The Most High, Mightie and Magnificent Empresse' Elizabeth:

If thou hast formed right true vertues face herein:
Vertue her selfe can best discerne, to whom they written
*   bin.*
If thou hast beautie praysd, let her sole lookes diuine
Iudge if ought therein be amis, and mend it by her eine.
If Chastitie want ought, or Temperance her dew,
Behold her Princely mind aright, and write thy Queene
*   anew.*

It was not difficult, with praise of his poem and talk of the court and the queen, and whither these things in conjunction might lead, to fire Spenser's mind, that had but smouldered in retirement; and thus it was, in the summer or fall of 1589, that the two men embarked together for England.

Perhaps Marlowe met Spenser on this famous visit (there is ample evidence that he already knew Raleigh) and saw the manuscript of *The Faerie Queene*. Two colorful passages and several lines from Spenser's poem found their way—from memory, and with changes—into the Second Part of *Tamburlaine*.

2.

Some of the evidence of Marlowe's acquaintance with the dark-haired Raleigh in his pearled and silver-gleaming garments may now be considered. It was about this time that Marlowe wrote a poem that can be mentioned on the same page with *The Faerie Queene*. It is interesting besides because it contains a hint—but no more—of a romantic attachment.

Scholars have evolved the thesis that much of the love poetry of the Elizabethans was composed as exercises in the art of verse—perhaps the art of pleasing, as well. It ought to be a simple matter to separate this kind of poetry from the other. . . .

To a young man of twenty-five, and a poet, an encounter—nay, sometimes merely a fleeting glimpse, if the image be but fair enough—is sufficient to evoke music from desire. Was this the catalyst that was at work when Marlowe sat down to write *The passionate Sheepheard to his loue?* Or was it indeed something more academic, that would bring this poem closer to the scholars' thesis, if not completely into its fold? For it echoes Ovid's *Metamorphoses,* the source also of a fifteenth century Spanish pastoral, which might have served as Marlowe's model. It is by Rodrigo Reinoso:

> I will give you painted shows,
> Fair striped kirtles,
> Caps as large
> As I can find.
>
> I will give you yellow ribbons
> Shoes, sandals, slippers;
> I will bring you a thousand marvels
> So there won't be your peer in the village.
>
> I will give you good gowns,
> Belts and girdles,
> So that amongst all the young girls
> There will be none to equal you.
>
> I will give you cheese and butter
> Which I have from my flock;
> I will make gittern-music
> For you to go dancing.[4]

Whatever the reason—his poem would justify almost any motivation, even that of imitation—one day he wrote:

Come liue with mee, and be my loue,
And we will all the pleasures proue,
That Vallies, groues, hills and fieldes,
Woods, or steepie mountaine yeeldes.

And we will sit vpon the Rocks,
Seeing the Sheepheards feede theyr flocks
By shallow Riuers, to whose falls
Melodious byrds sing Madrigalls.

And I will make thee beds of Roses,
And a thousand fragrant poesies,
A cap of flowers, and a kirtle,
Imbroydred all with leaues of Mirtle.

A gowne made of the finest wooll,
Which from our pretty Lambes we pull,
Fayre lined slippers for the cold,
With buckles of the purest gold.

A belt of straw and Iuie buds,
With Corall clasps and Amber studs,
And if these pleasures may thee moue,
Come liue with mee, and be my loue.

The Sheepheards Swaines shall daunce & sing
For thy delight each May-morning.
If these delights thy minde may moue,
Then liue with mee, and be my loue.

And being twenty-five, and a poet, he showed the
verses to his friends. Raleigh has recorded his familiarity
with them in *The Nimphs Reply to the Sheepheard:*

A most excellent Ditty of the
Louers promises to his beloued.
To a sweet new tune, called,
Liue with me and be my Loue.

The Ladies prudent answer to
her Loue.
To the same tune.

Liue with me and be my Loue,
And we will all the pleasures proue,
That Vallies, Groues, Hills, and Fields,
Woods, or steepy Mountaines yeelds:
  That Valleys, Groues, Hils, and Fields,
  Woods, or steepy Mountaines yeelds.

And we will sit vpon the Rockes,
Seeing the Shepheards feede their flockes
By shallow Riuers to whose falls,
Melodious Birds sing Madrigals,
  by shallow riuers to whose fals, &c.

And I will make thee beds of Roses,
And a thousand fragrant Poses:
A Cap of Flowers and a Kirtle,
Imbrodred all with leaues of Mirtle,
  a Cap of Flowers and a Kirtle, &c.

A Gowne made of the finest Wooll,
Which from our pretty Lambs we pull:
Faire lined Slippers for the cold,
With buckles of the purest Gold:
  faire lined Slippers for the cold, &c.

Thy siluer dishes fild with meate,
As pretious as the Gods doe eate,
Shall on an Iuory Table be,
Prepar'd each day for thee and me,
  shall on an Iuory table be, &c.

The Shepheards swaines shall dance & sing
For thy delight each faire morning:
If these delights thy minde might mooue,
To liue with me and be my loue,
  if these delights, &c.   FINIS.

If all the world and Loue were young,
And truth in euery Shepheards tongue:
These pretty pleasures might me mooue,
To liue with thee and be thy loue,
  these pretty pleasures, &c.

But flowers fade, and wanton Fields,
To wayward Winter reckning yeelds,
A hony tongue, a heart of gall,
Is fancies spring, but sorrowes fall.
  a hony tongue, &c.

Time driues the Flocks from field to fold,
When riuers rage and Rockes grow cold:
And Philomel becommeth dumbe,
The rest complaines of cares to come.
  and Philomel becommeth, &c.

Thy Gownes, thy shooes, thy beds of roses,
Thy cap, thy kirtle and thy poses:
Soone breakes, soone withers, soone forgot,
In folly ripe, in reason rotten.   (ten.
  soone breakes, &c.

What should you talke of dainties then,
Of better meate then serueth men:
All that is vaine, this onely good,
Which God doth blesse and send for food,
  all that is vaine, &c.

If you could last and loue still breede,
Had ioyes no date, nor age no neede,
Then these delights my mind might mooue,
To liue with thee and be thy Loue.
  then these delights, &c.
Printed by the Assignes of Thomas symcock

'A sweet new tune:

Liue with me and be my loue.'

If all the world and loue were young,
And truth in euery Sheepheards tongue,
These pretty pleasures might me moue,
To liue with thee, and be thy loue.

Time driues the flocks from field to fold,
When Riuers rage, and Rocks grow cold,
And Philomell becommeth dombe,
The rest complaines of cares to come.

The flowers doe fade, and wanton fieldes,
To wayward winter reckoning yeeldes,
A honny tongue, a hart of gall,
Is fancies spring, but sorrowes fall.

Thy gownes, thy shooes, thy beds of Roses,
Thy cap, thy kirtle, and thy poesies,
Soone breake, soone wither, soone forgotten:
In follie ripe, in reason rotten.

Thy belt of straw and Iuie buddes,
Thy Corall claspes and Amber studdes,
All these in mee no meanes can moue,
To come to thee, and be thy loue.

But could youth last, and loue still breede,
Had ioyes no date, nor age no neede,
Then these delights my minde might moue,
To liue with thee, and be thy loue.

Thenceforward, first for their own circle, but afterwards
for all the world, Marlowe's poem and his were linked
together: the invitation to love, and love's answer, full of

wisdom. Donne, Herrick and Cotton wrote imitations of *The Passionate Sheepheard*; and it was in their time that Izaak Walton's incomparable praise appeared: 'Her voice was good, and the Ditty fitted for it; 'twas that smooth song which was made by *Kit. Marlow,* now at least fifty years ago: and the milk-maids Mother sung an answer to it, which was made by Sir *Walter Raleigh* in his younger days. They were old fashioned Poetry, but choicely good, I think much better than the strong lines that are now in fashion in this critical age.' [5]

3.

It was unfortunate for Marlowe in the end that his dealings with Raleigh were not confined to poetry. A more sinister relationship—I give the view of contemporaries—existed.

At Raleigh's dwelling in Durham House, once the town house of the See of Durham, seized by the crown in Edward VI's days, relinquished by Mary, and resumed by Elizabeth for disposal to her favorites, there gathered a group of men with probing minds—scientists, scholars, poets. One of the most remarkable members of this remarkable group was Thomas Harriot, [6] Raleigh's mathematical tutor and devoted friend, a scholar and scientist who had made important astronomical discoveries; who wrote *A briefe and true report of the new found land of Virginia* (he had been a member of Raleigh's first colonization party), and who was the inventor of the telescope (the honor, in any case, appears to be evenly divided between him and Galileo, who was experimenting with long-distance lenses at the same time). Other members included Henry Percy, ninth Earl of Northumberland, Raleigh's fellow-prisoner in the Tower in the dark days to come; Walter Warner, a mathematician, and the poets George Chapman and Matthew Roydon.

In the privacy of Raleigh's study overlooking the Thames, the incense of tobacco smoke rising from little silver pipes, lively, occasionally blasphemous, discussions were carried on. Astronomy, the chronology of Genesis, the search for an elixir, the nature of the soul, were some of the subjects that engrossed them. Marlowe, the erstwhile divinity student, entertained them with an 'atheist lecture' in which he contended, among other things: 'That the Jndians and many Authors of antiquity haue assuredly writen of aboue 16 thowsand yeares agone whereas Adam is proued to haue lived within 6 thowsand yeares. . . . That Moyses made the Jewes to travell xl yeares in the wildernes, (which Jorney might haue bin done in lesse then one yeare) ere they Came to the promised land to thintent that those who were privy to most of his subtilties might perish and so an everlasting superstition Remain in the hartes of the people. . . . That the first beginning of Religioun was only to keep men in awe.'

He even bragged 'That if he were put to write a new Religion, he would vndertake both a more Exellent and Admirable methode and that all the new testament is filthily written,' and recklessly went around saying 'That Moyses was but a Jugler & that one Heriots being Sir W Raleighs man Can do more then he.' [7]

Part of this may have been self-justification for turning his back on divinity. Yet why Marlowe should have found it necessary to blurt such things out—as he did all his life —is a mystery. Was he unsure, and did he find in this a compensation for uncertainty? Or did he enjoy the perilous thrill of gazing on the abyss and seeing how far he could descend without hurtling down? For presently there were reports 'Of Sir Walter Rawley's schoole of Atheisme by the waye, & of the Conjurer that is Master thereof, and of the diligence vsed to get yong gentlemen of this schoole, where in both Moyses, & our Sauior, the olde, and the new Testamente are iested at, and the schollers taughte amonge other thinges, to spell God backwarde;'[8] while Nashe sneered in print: 'I heare say there be Mathematicians abroad, that will proue men before *Adam*.'[9]

It was no jesting matter when the authorities, spiritual and temporal, got wind of it.

CHAPTER XII

Marlowe's Mighty Line [1]

I.

THEY are showing *Doctor Faustus* at the Rose theater across the Thames in Southwark. By ferry, and
by foot over London Bridge, the people throng to it—
as the preacher at Paul's Cross saith: 'Will not a filthy
play, with the blast of a trumpet, sooner call thither a
thousand, than an hour's tolling of a bell bring to the
sermon a hundred?'

A trumpet lifts the heart; a bell tolls gloom. The
trumpeter at the Rose sends yellow slivers of sound pierc-
ing into the air to announce that the show is on, and for a
few minutes an intimate hurly-burly possesses the spectators as they troop to their places. The scene has been described thus: 'In our assemblies at plays in London, you
shall see such heaving, and shoving, such itching and
shouldering, to sit by women: such care for their garments, that they be not trod on: such eyes to their laps,
that no chips light in them: such pillows to their backs,
that they get no hurt: such masking in their ears, I know
not what: such giving them pippins to pass the time: such
playing at foot-saunt without cards: such tickling, such
toying, such smiling, such winking, and such manning

THE
TRAGICALL

History of D. Faustus.

As it hath bene Acted by the Right
Honorable the Earle of Nottingham his seruants.

Written by Ch. Marl.

LONDON

Printed by V. S, for Thomas Bushell. 1604.

them home, when the sports are ended, that it is a right comedy to mark their behavior.' [2]

The Rose is a circular building on which a flag flutters to tell all who look in its direction that a performance is scheduled. Its stage, thrusting deep into the audience, is bare save for a table piled with folios. Garbed in a flowing university gown, Edward Alleyn enters. He is Faustus. The theater turns quiet.

Alleyn is Faustus, but he is also Marlowe: Marlowe's *persona*. He begins his soliloquy in Cambridge terms, asking aloud the questions Marlowe had asked himself a thousand times in the old storehouse chamber at Corpus Christi, until resolution came, until theology had been rejected for a life of authorship—and with it the other faculties of the university: law, medicine and the liberal arts.

The merged divinity student—Marlowe projected in Faustus—begins to probe himself:

> Settle thy studies *Faustus*, and beginne
> To sound the deapth of that thou wilt professe:
> Hauing commencde, be a Diuine in shew,
> Yet leuell at the end of euery Art,
> And liue and die in *Aristotles* workes.

We are back in the shadow of the Old Court, Corpus Christi, as Marlowe was in mood and memory when he wrote this, raising the warring factions of his mind to bring them to order again as he did in the crisis of 1587. Divinity is a lost cause; the other faculties offer little:

> Is to dispute well, Logickes chiefest end,
> Affoords this Art no greater myracle?
> Then reade no more, thou hast attaind the end.

He leaves the liberal arts to ponder the role of physician, but mortality stands in the way of great achievement, and again he rejects a potential pursuit:

> Wouldst thou make man to liue eternally?
> Or being dead, raise them to life againe?
> Then this profession were to be esteemed.
> Physicke farewell, where is *Iustinian?*

He calls up the person of the great lawgiver, only to decide that Law is

> A petty case of paltry legacies,

and, as a profession,

> Too seruile and illiberall for me.

He is back at the starting point, and once more, as of old, he must dispose of the profession for which his training has fitted him:

> When all is done, Diuinitie is best.
> *Ieromes* Bible, *Faustus,* view it well.
> *Stipendium peccati mors est:* ha, *Stipendium, &c.*
> The reward of sinne is death: thats hard.

He has come across something to give him pause; the sign that might keep him steadfast to his early vows is not vouchsafed him:

> If we say that we haue no sinne,
> We deceiue our selues, and theres no truth in vs.
> Why then belike
> We must sinne, and so consequently die.
> I, we must die an euerlasting death:
> What doctrine call you this, *Che sera, sera,*
> What wil be, shall be? Diuinitie, adieu.

Thus far Marlowe, bringing to the Rose the echoes of old disputations in his mind. He had chosen authorship; Faustus chooses magic. As Alleyn comes to the business of the play, the audience leans forward:

> Lines, circles, sceanes, letters and characters:
> I, these are those that *Faustus* most desires.
> O what a world of profit and delight,
> Of power, of honor, of omnipotence
> Is promised to the studious Artizan?
> All things that mooue betweene the quiet poles.

2.

Wagging finger, gaping mouth—all the pious palaver that the Dark Ages had added to this story of a man's compact with the devil, of which every town and hamlet in Europe had its didactic example, is about to be swept aside by one who has no moral to point, no sermon to preach; whose business is poetry, not the putative salvation of souls. Now, for the first time since he was conjured out of cringing speech, Faustus is a hero to his creator, and the play about him, clad in the splendor of Marlowe's verse, glows against the medieval night. Alleyn's audience has sharp, attentive ears for the rapturous lines: it is a simpler day than ours, and a simpler folk that hearkens.

Faustus is resolved:

> Tis Magicke, Magicke that hath rauisht mee.

He consults two famous dabblers in the forbidden art, and is promised, if he is resolute, dominion over 'the subiects of euery element':

> Like Lyons shall they guard vs when we please,
> Like *Almaine* Rutters with their horsemens staues,
> Or Lapland Gyants trotting by our sides—

(as Marlowe wrote this, two lines from *Tamburlaine* came back to him—

> So lookes my Loue, shadowing in her browes
> Triumphes and Trophees for my victories,

to be miraculously transformed to,

> Sometimes like women, or vnwedded maides,
> Shadowing more beautie in their ayrie browes,
> Then haue the white breasts of the queene of Loue.)

Thus flattered, Faustus replies:

ere I sleepe Ile trie what I can do,
This night Ile coniure though I die therefore.

Alleyn As Faustus, Devil As Devil

There is an edition of the play, the title-page of which
is adorned with a woodcut showing Faustus on the stage

in a magician's circle, conjuring book in one hand, a staff in the other, and a devil beginning to rise through the trapdoor at his words:

> Within this circle is *Iehouahs* name,
> Forward and backward anagrammatiz'd
> The breuiated names of holy Saints,
> Figures of euery adiunct to the heauens,
> And characters of signes and erring starres.

There is a thunderclap; out of terror and darkness the first devil appears, and Faustus starts back, exclaiming:

> I charge thee to returne and chaunge thy shape,
> Thou art too vgly to attend on me.

Mephistopheles is more subtle; he enters next, and with him Faustus disputes as he would with a fellow scholar, in dialogue reminiscent of the parleys between Job and Elihu, and Job and the Lord, in the Old Testament.

Their disputation ends on a sublime philosophical note:

> Where are you damn'd?

> In hell.

> How comes it then that thou art out of hel?

> Why this is hel, nor am I out of it.

3.

The twenty-four years of his compact have run their course. He has performed notable feats, and he has conversed with the high, illustrious dead. But it has not been smugness in his heart and quiet in his mind, as perhaps it was not in Marlowe's. His latest creator has molded Faustus in his own image:

> I do repent, and yet I do dispaire:
> Hell striues with grace for conquest in my breast,
> What shal I do to shun the snares of death?

These thoughts arouse the ire of Mephistopheles; Faustus pleads for pardon and a final boon:

> One thing, good seruant, let me craue of thee,
> To glut the longing of my hearts desire,
> That I might haue vnto my paramour,
> That heauenly *Helen* which I saw of late.

It is the executioner's grant to the doomed prisoner:

> *Enter Helen.*
> Was this the face that lancht a thousand shippes?
> And burnt the toplesse Towres of Ilium?
> Sweete *Helen*, make me immortall with a kisse:
> Her lips sucke forth my soule, see where it flies:
> Come *Helen*, come giue mee my soule againe.

Here wil I dwel, for heauen be in these lips,
And all is drosse that is not *Helena*.

Like Marlowe in the fleet, fused moments when he
wrote this, Faustus has regained his lost heaven in Helen's
beauty, and he is loath to leave off praising the radiance
which has sublimated him, for darkness and doom wait at
the end. The music rises and beats with a more passionate
accent; it is the ancient and immortal lyric voice of man
proffering worlds to Beauty's Queen:

I wil be *Paris*, and for loue of thee,
Insteede of *Troy* shal *Wertenberge* be sackt,
And I wil combate with weake *Menelaus*,
And weare thy colours on my plumed Crest:
Yea I wil wound *Achillis* in the heele,
And then returne to *Helen* for a kisse.

And still the 'quenchles fire' of Marlowe's protagonist
blazes forth to light the depths of the Rose with mystical
splendor:

O thou art fairer then the euening aire,
Clad in the beauty of a thousand starres,
Brighter art thou then flaming *Iupiter*,
When he appeared to haplesse *Semele*,
More louely then the monarke of the skie
In wanton *Arethusaes* azurde armes.

It is the quintessence of worship and praise, the ulti-
mate homage to the ideal of sacred and profane love that

through all ages has made men fare forth lonely, on horse
and on foot, to seek out beauty under the sky and in the
beautiful cities of the world. It is the burden of their
verse—Milton's

> With thee conversing I forget all time

(and the Lady of Christ's College learned much and took
much from Marlowe's blank verse); and

> Though the whole world run rack
> And go dark with cloud,
> Light is
> Where she stands,

by Cerclamon; [3] and John Lydgate's

> Queene of Heaven, of Hell eke Emperess,
> Lady of this world, O very Lodestar,

echoed in Villon's

> Dame du ciel, regente terrienne,
> Emperiere des infernaux palus.

It is Jonson's

> The world may find the spring by following her,

and Campion's

Follow your saint, follow with accents sweet!
Haste you, sad notes, fall at her flying feet!

and Donne's

By our first strange and fatal interview,
By all desires which thereof did ensue—

the brief, yet immortal grace conferred by love on men
and monumented in their song, the bright words flashing
like larks against encompassing night.

4.

To the spectators at the Rose, it is the interlude before
annihilation. Terror waits offstage, and they know and
fear it. The doom brought upon Faustus by his own deed
is swift and implacable, but it is shadowed forth by Marlowe in human terms, not vindictive moralizing—the
modern man is speaking from the medieval maze.

For the last time Faustus meets his fellow scholars. A
sigh is his salutation; their words create the mood:

Ah Gentlemen!

What ailes Faustus?

Ah my sweete chamber-fellow! had I liued with thee,
then had I liued stil, but now I die eternally: looke,
comes he not? comes he not?

Remembrances of things past, regrets and despair, well up in him. He tells his story, and their hearts leap with the rabbit Terror. The scholars depart, leaving Faustus alone with his fate. Expectation hushes the Rose; the lone figure on the stage is silent. Suddenly: '*The clocke strikes eleauen.*' It is the peal of doom. The death agony begins:

> Ah Faustus,
> Now hast thou but one bare hower to liue,
> And then thou must be damnd perpetually:
> Stand stil you euer moouing spheres of heauen,
> That time may cease, and midnight neuer come:
> Faire Natures eie, rise, rise againe, and make
> Perpetuall day, or let this houre be but
> A yeere, a moneth, a weeke, a naturall day,
> That Faustus may repent, and saue his soule,
> *O lente, lente curite noctis equi*—

it is a line remembered from Ovid in the lonely storehouse chamber long ago, the cry of the lover in Corinna's arms —'O slowly, slowly gallop, horses of the night'—the plea of the hour of joy in the hour of doom. But relentlessly:

> The starres mooue stil, time runs, the clocke wil strike,
> The diuel wil come, and Faustus must be damned.

Alleyn, alone on the stage, as in the beginning, is now a magician of harmonies, uttering the broken rhythms of Marlowe's verse to crowd an hour's agony into fifty-nine lines:

O Ile leape vp to my God: who pulles me downe?
See see where Christs blood streams in the firmament.
One drop would saue my soule, halfe a drop, ah my
    Christ.
Ah rend not my heart for naming of my Christ,
Yet wil I call on him: oh spare me *Lucifer!*

The clock strikes; there is thunder and lightning; the
devils enter to bear him away:

Adders, and Serpents, let me breathe a while:
Vgly hell gape not, come not *Lucifer,*
Ile burne my bookes, ah *Mephastophilis.*[4]

The play is done. In the balcony, gentlemen and their
ladies set their hats atilt, ruffs are smoothed out, cloaks
fastened. Below, the groundlings begin to mill and stream
forth, bound for Bankside wharves where the watermen
wait, bound for London Bridge and the city and the workaday world, their awed whispers starting the legend of
Satan himself appearing in the midst of devils capering
excitedly on the stage. Past the houses of prostitution in
fee to the Bishop of Winchester, past the waterside epis-
copal palace called Winchester House, they make their
way, but not boisterously as is their wont after a performance. Behind them, in the emptying Rose, Henslowe com-
putes his profits.

CHAPTER XIII

Marlowe's Table Talk

I.

DOCTOR FAUSTUS marks the flood tide of Marlowe's genius. Whether he lived to write more, or died at twenty-six, the light of glory would lie upon the pages of his work forever. Now, for a certainty, it could be said,

>   his raptures were
> All ayre, and fire;

progressively, from his school-day translations to *Tamburlaine*, from *Tamburlaine* to *Doctor Faustus*, his verse had grown in subtlety and power until, by the end of 1590, no other writer's work could compare with his for vision and splendor of diction. He had created a masterpiece, the lot of few makers.

Had this triumph marked the end of his career, or of our knowledge of his life, our vision of him would have been a more dazzling one. It was not to be. Another side of Marlowe, irreconcilable with our earlier concepts, presents itself by the following year.

In 1591, Marlowe was sharing a chamber in London with Thomas Kyd. What month it was, what season of the year, or how long their association lasted, we do not know, for that is the way of Marlowe's life; but we may assume, from the circumstances, that the two men were writing for the same theatrical company. What Marlowe's play was is another matter—perhaps *The Jew of Malta,* which fits this period in his development and shows the marks of a second, less skillful, more sensational hand: I think Kyd's. But all that can be said with certainty is that they were working together some time in 1591; we know this because Kyd, in trouble in 1593, found it necessary to hark back to Marlowe and this 'occasion of our wrytinge in one chamber twoe yeares synce.'

Kyd, in 1591, was in the service of a pious nobleman who was also the patron of a company of actors. He is otherwise unidentified. The Admiral's men, for whom Marlowe had been writing, appear to have joined forces, or merged, at this time with Lord Strange's men. Since it was Lord Strange's company that produced both *The Spanish Tragedie* and *The Jew of Malta*—significant conjunction—I assume Ferdinando Stanley, Lord Strange, to have been the man.[1] If Marlowe was in his employ at this time, it was merely as a writer for his company. Kyd's position seems to have been different; he was a member of his master's household, perhaps as secretary to his lordship.

This much we learn from the two records Kyd has left of his unhappy association with Marlowe. Although the records belong to the year 1593, when Kyd was on the threshold of oblivion, both refer to the period of writing together in 1591, when Marlowe entered his life. How

did Marlowe, Marlowe the famous progenitor of *Faustus*
and *Tamburlaine*, appear to Kyd at that time? The dim
portrait of our author is about to darken. In the depositions of Kyd we have a view of Marlowe such as we do
not otherwise possess, a portrait that comes to life through
speech and characterization, done with all the cunning of
a dramatist who has lived on intimate terms with his subject; through Kyd, we seem to hear Marlowe speak. That
the things he quotes Marlowe as uttering are not pleasant
to hear is another matter. One, at least, must have been
droll in the telling; but the humor, like the ink with
which it was written, has somewhat faded: 'ffirst it was his
custom when I knewe him first & as I heare saie he contynewd it in table talk or otherwise to iest at the devine
scriptures gybe at praiers, & stryve in argument to frustrate & confute what hath byn spoke or wrytt by prophets
& such holie menn.

  '1. He would report St John to be our savior Christes
Alexis I cover it with reverence and trembling that is that
Christ did loue him with an extraordinary loue.

  '2. That for me to wryte a poem of St *paules* conversion as I was determined he said wold be as if I shold go
wryte a book of fast & loose, esteeming *Paul* a Jugler.

  '3. That the prodigall Childes portion was but fower
nobles, he held his purse so neere the bottom in all pictures, and that it either was a iest or els fowr nobles then
was thought a great patrimony not thinking it a parable.

  '4. That things esteemed to be donn by devine power
might haue aswell been don by observation of men all
which he wold so sodenlie take slight occasion to slyp out

as I & many others in regard of his other rashnes in attempting soden pryvie iniuries to men did ouerslypp thogh often reprehend him for it & for which god is my witnes aswell by my lordes comaundment as in hatred of his life & thoughts I left & did refraine his companie.'[2]

Even in the indirect quotation, the turn of phrase that was Marlowe's breaks through. His rebuff to Kyd, who piously proposed to write a poem on St. Paul, recalls his earlier outburst concerning the Rev. Richard Harvey, in Nashe's memorandum. Marlowe was intolerant; he was also reckless. Perhaps he felt secure, in the circles in which he was a noted figure, from the hounding of the religious who stood, vigilant and limned in flame, on the margin of men's thoughts. As for his 'other rashnes in attempting soden pryvie iniuries to men'—what can this mean but that Marlowe, losing his temper, lashed out in rage with fists instead of words? It is not pretty.

Kyd leaves no doubt of his distate; and he has managed to characterize himself, too. Less spirited than his fellow writer; less brilliant, less inspired; outwardly circumspect and pious, Kyd reports his association with Marlowe as a cruel and humiliating experience. There is an unhappy ring to his indictment which is convincing. They came together without friendship, and parted with hatred—at least, on Kyd's side. Kyd never forgave his chamber fellow for what he was made to endure. Worse, when he thought it might be useful to him in his dire need two years later, he set his complaints (and accusations) down —he blabbed and calumniated.

The two men might have talked occasionally about the

poetry of their time, the theater, the merits of contemporaries—the youth from Stratford, for example; but if they did, Kyd does not mention it. He might have left such a record of Marlowe as Drummond left of Jonson, as Jonson and Fuller left of Shakespeare. His experience made it impossible.

Much may be forgiven him. When, in 1593, soul shaken, broken by torture, blinded by bitterness, he lashed out at Marlowe, the impress of their association was still almost more than he could bear, even in recollection. The second of his two records belongs to that part of the story, and it will be found there.

2.

It was early in 1592 that *The Jew of Malta* was presented at the Rose by Lord Strange's men, with Edward Alleyn in the title role. The company's repertory included Kyd's *Spanish Tragedie*, Greene's *Friar Bacon and Friar Bungay*, and the First Part of *Henry VI*.

For this production of *The Jew*, in the purlieus of Southwark, Marlowe wrote a Prologue, spoken by the spirit of Machiavelli, which contains a passage that appears to be autobiographical. It is possible that it refers to his recent association with Kyd, although he had ill-wishers enough to choose from for a retort from the stage; considering Greene's early attack on him, and his subsequent imitation of Marlowe's work, the passage might apply to Greene as well as to Kyd:

To some perhaps my name is odious,
But such as loue me, gard me from their tongues,
And let them know that I am *Macheuill*,
And weigh not men, and therefore not mens words:
Admir'd I am of those that hate me most.
Though some speake openly against my bookes,
Yet will they reade me.

This contained a double boast. *Il Principe* of Machiavelli was being read in England—if Marlowe did not
know Italian, he appears nevertheless to have picked up
much of the Italian's matter in conversation—and the
Prologue was a convenient way of showing his familiarity
with it.

The idea for Marlowe's play might have been sug-
gested by the story of a Portuguese Jew who fled from
persecution in Europe to the court of the Sultan Selim in
Constantinople.[3] He was a member of the famous Nassi
family, converts to Christianity who in their own hearts
and homes nourished the flickering flame of Judaism with
their sufferings. As a governor and administrator under
the Sultan, Nassi prospered, becoming at length Duke of
Naxos and the Cyclades—Naxos, isle of fruit and wine,
and all those islands set like jewels in the Mediterranean
on the flank of Asia Minor's thrust towards Europe. So
powerful did he become that he even coined his own
money, inscribed 'Josephus Naci Dei Gratia Dux Pelagi'
—'by the grace of God Duke of the Archipelago.' But
even when we learn that Nassi brought about the Turkish
attack on Cyprus in 1570, the resemblance between him

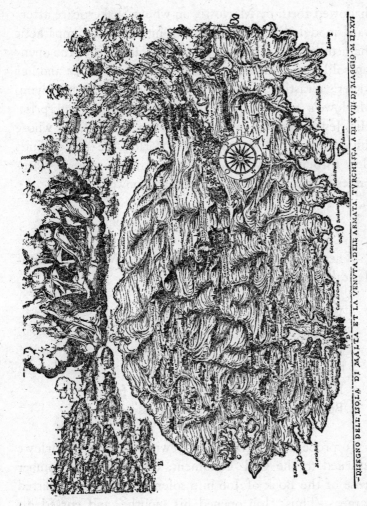

‐RISEGNO DELL·ISOLA·DI MALTA·ET·LA VENVTA·DELL·ARMATA TVRCHESCA·A·DI X VIII·DI MAGGIO·M·DLXVI‐

The Turks Attack Malta

and Barabas of Malta remains ephemeral. The Jew shadowed forth by Marlowe, on whom Shakespeare afterward modeled his Shylock, is an intense and sympathetic characterization. The language of Barabas, from the opening soliloquy until he becomes a caricature under another writer's recasting, is full of dignity and poetry, embodying Marlowe's never-ebbing delight in fabulous enterprise. His Jew talks like a rich Renaissance merchant whose ships toss in the waters of the world; the trade winds blow through his words, bright with the jewels of place-names, strong with the opulence and power of

> Infinite riches in a little roome.

When Barabas speaks for his race, Marlowe's anti-clerical attitude helps him:

> Who hateth me but for my happinesse?
> Or who is honour'd now but for his wealth?
> Rather had I a Iew be hated thus,
> Then pittied in a Christian pouerty:
> For I can see no fruits in all their faith,
> But malice, falshood, and excessiue pride.

To probe the depths of the Jewish character, Marlowe returned to the Old Testament, translating the somber prose of the Book of Job into solemn iambics for afflicted Barabas. Thus, 'Iob opened his mouthe, and cursed his day. And Iob cryed out, and said, Let the daye perish, wherein I was borne, and the night when it was said,

There is a manchilde conceiued. Let yt day be darknes,' becomes in the *Jew of Malta:*

> but I may curse the day,
> Thy fatall birth-day, forlorne *Barabas;*
> And henceforth wish for an eternall night,
> That clouds of darkenesse may inclose my flesh;

and the three Jews who turn to Barabas in their common peril are the three Job-comforters of the Bible dramatized.

Over all is the moral burden from the pages of the Old Testament, epitomized by Barabas in a single line:

> The man that dealeth righteously shall liue—

a concept which Marlowe had himself expressed earlier (in *Tamburlaine*) as

> Vertue solely is the sum of glorie.

There is a later play that ranks higher in the canon of Marlowe's works, but none shows better how he might have developed, how mature his thoughts and emotion could become, than this one, fragmentary and garbled as it is in the version we possess. For there is more here than mere anticlericalism. There is the deep humanity of the true genius, such as we find in Shakespeare. For Marlowe, no less than Shakespeare, despite deep-rooted antagonisms, was concerned with the disparity between Christian precepts and Christian practice—religious wars, and piety serving pillage:

What? bring you Scripture to confirm your wrongs?

I have referred to a fumbling, sensational hand present in the text of Marlowe's play. There is no other way to account for the sudden change from drama to melodrama which finally overwhelms the structure of *The Jew of Malta*, as rising waters might first flood, then submerge a pillared edifice. Marlowe leaves Barabas noble in adversity, looking to heaven to right his wrongs—

Oh thou that with a fiery piller led'st
The sonnes of *Israel* through the dismall shades,
Light *Abrahams* off-spring—

while another brings him back a monster of revenge who boasts

I walke abroad a nights
And kill sicke people groaning under walls:
Sometimes I goe about and poyson wells—

the opening of a long catalogue of crimes in the somber rhythms of *The Spanish Tragedie*. The conjecture is irresistable that Marlowe was dismissed by Lord Strange after his opinions became known; and as the play he was working on was the property of Strange's company, he left it behind, unfinished, when his employment ceased.

The memory of Marlowe, as much as of Marlowe's Jew, moved Shakespeare when he penned *The Merchant of Venice*. That sweet song, sung whilst Bassanio comments on the caskets, and indeed the whole scene in which it is imbedded, is full of the imagery and rhythms of *Hero and Leander;* while in an earlier scene Shakespeare transforms his Prince of Morocco into a Tamburlaine:

> The Hyrcanian deserts and the vasty wilds
> Of wide Arabia are as thoroughfares now
> For princes to come view fair Portia:
> The watery kingdom, whose ambitious head
> Spits in the face of heaven, is no bar
> To stop the foreign spirits, but they come,
> As o'er a brook, to see fair Portia.

The resemblances between Barabas and Shylock, their daughters Abigail and Jessica; Marlowe's 'Oh my girle, my gold,' and Shakespeare's 'My daughter! O my ducats!'; the daughters' Christian lovers, and, finally, Marlowe's

> But stay, what starre shines yonder in the *East?*
> The Loadstarre of my life, if *Abigall,*

remembered for Romeo:

> But, soft! what light through yonder window breaks?
> It is the east, and Juliet is the sun,

are perhaps too well known for further comment.

The play ran intermittently at the Rose from 1592 to 1596, with a revival in 1601, and exceeded by eleven performances the representations of *Dr. Faustus*. No sixteenth century edition has come down to us, although the Stationers' Register reveals that *the famouse tregedie of the Riche Jewe of Malta* was entered for publication May 17, 1594, a year after Marlowe's death. Fire and water, fishmongers and trunk-makers, apparently did for it.

CHAPTER XIV

Marlowe and the Constables

I.

ROARING drunkenly homeward in the month of
May, 1592, Christopher Marlowe collided with
Allen Nicholls, constable of Shoreditch, and Nicholas
Helliot, under-constable. Perhaps he assaulted them, thus
confirming Kyd's accusation about Marlowe's 'rashnes in
attempting soden pryvie iniuries to men.' Frowsy heads
of queans popped from the doors and windows of Holywell Street—behind them, peering hard, their soldier or
actor clients. They saw the celebrated poet in the toils of
the law—again.

But if this is not what happened, what was it? For once
again, with Marlowe in trouble, we get some trace of him.
Somewhere in the dusty Elizabethan records there may
be a sequel; but it could not have been a serious one,
albeit for the moment he is once more under arrest.

Sir Owen Hopton, Justice and Lieutenant of the Tower,
looks up and meets the eyes of an old acquaintance. He
listens to the complaints of the constables, and prepares
the usual formula for the courts. Recollecting that in three
years Marlowe has progressed from suspicion of murder
to disorderly conduct, he may have considered wryly that
the young man who stands before him is virtually on the

137

road to respectability. Nevertheless, the charge is sufficiently grave, and the forms must be observed.

Therefore he gives the prisoner a talking to and extracts a promise: 'Middlesex ss. Memorandum that on the ixth day of May, 1592, the xxxiiijth Year of the Reign of our lady Elizabeth Now &c, there appeared before me, Owen Hopton, Knight, one of the Justices of the said lady Queen, assigned to Keep the peace in the aforesaid county, Christopher Marle of London, gentleman, and acknowledged that he owed the said lady Queen xx pounds in good and lawful English money: Upon Condition that he will personally appear at the next general Session of the peace held in and for the aforesaid county: and meanwhile will keep the peace towards the whole people of the said lady Queen and especially towards Allen Nicholls, Constable, of Hollowwellstreet in the aforesaid county, and Nicholas Helliott, underconstable of the same: Which sum aforesaid he permits to be raised for the use of the said lady Queen in the form of a Recognizance, from his goods, and Chattle lands and tenements If he should fail in his promise.' [1]

Marlowe is twenty-eight, and promises are as easy to hand out as money for the pleasures of this world. The next General Sessions, at which he is to appear, are five months distant, an eternity. The constables are appeased, and Marlowe bids them and Sir Owen adieu. Sober now —soberer, in any case—he strolls back to his lodgings, eager to recount the adventure to his friend.

There are shrieks of laughter at the discomfiture of the police, and perhaps additional merriment in the account

Marlowe has brought back of Sir Owen Hopton, whom Watson also has met.

2.

Marlowe, at this time, among other affairs, was occupied with a play which has reached posterity in a sad state of garble, *The Massacre at Paris: With the Death of the Duke of Guise.*

The Guise, as Henslowe labeled it in his wretched diary scrawl, fits the Marlovian pattern of a protagonist with an aspiring mind. Across the Channel, the journey of a day, the clock went back a century or more—and still does in that brief, perilous crossing; and there, within the walls of Paris, he depicted the monster of his youth who had filled Canterbury with Protestant refugees telling and retelling the story of St. Bartholomew's Eve. England, like Walsingham, had never forgotten. The results, outside of France, were like those of the Nazi excesses, of more recent memory. The English wanted the Treaty of Blois torn up and the French ambassador driven out. For weeks after the massacre Elizabeth refused him an audience, and when he finally was admitted to her presence, he found the entire court dressed in mourning. Like the apologists for Hitler, he dwelt on the necessity of swift, ruthless action in defense of the realm, and mumbled, distraught and embarrassed under the freezing stare of the Protestant queen, about ungovernable mob fury, as though it had been a spontaneous outbreak that had almost annihilated a religious minority.

THE
MASSACRE
AT PARIS:

With the Death of the Duke
of Guise.

As it was plaide by the right honourable the
Lord high *Admirall* his Seruants.

Written by *Christopher Marlow,*

AT LONDON
Printed by *E. A.* for *Edward White*, dwelling neere
the little North doore of S. Paules
Church, at the signe of
the Gun.

At the table of Thomas Walsingham, Marlowe would have heard much about the haughty duke whose private army menaced his sovereign and who, save for differences of birth, looms in the twentieth century mind as a Renaissance Hitler:

> Guise, weare our crowne, and be thou King of France,
> And as Dictator make or warre or peace,
> Whilst I cry *placet* like a Senator,

Henry exclaims. And like all the others in Marlowe's canon, the chief actor mounts in his hour of somber glory only to fall at the end. Now he sounds the tocsin of ambition:

> Oft haue I leueld, and at last haue learned,
> That perill is the cheefest way to happines,
> And resolution honors fairest aime.

It is the voice of the superman, 'live dangerously,' who uses religion to further his own ends, and whose denominational leadership is a device of policy. It is Guise who utters Marlowe's antireligious credo—it was safe:

> Religion: *O Diabole.*
> Fye, I am ashamde, how euer that I seeme,
> To think a word of such a simple sound
> Of so great matter should be made the ground.

Indeed, in this play, more than elsewhere in his extant writings, Marlowe's antireligious fury sweeps the stage like a whirlwind. With bolder strokes he projects the plotters of St. Bartholomew's Eve to hold the horror-stricken gaze of his English audience while he dins into English ears his scorn of popery, i.e., religion. And, recalling the rumors that went the rounds when he absented himself from Cambridge five years before, rumors that had him seeking sanctuary in Rheims or Rome, he takes this occasion to even matters up.

The horrors of the massacre that choked the Seine with corpses are occasionally relieved by Marlowe's humor— grim, but effective. Thus, when Ramus, professor of logic at the Sorbonne, falls into the hands of Guise and his bigots, they have a disputation:

Wherein hath *Ramus* been so offencious?

the cringing professor asks, and Guise replies:

Marry sir, in hauing a smack in all,
And yet didst neuer sound anything to the depth.
Was it not thou that scoftes the Organon,
And said it was a heape of vanities?
He that will be a flat dicotamest,
And seen in nothing but Epitomies:
Is in your iudgment thought a learned man.
And he forsooth must goe and preach in Germany:
Excepting against Doctors axioms,
And *ipse dixi* with this quidditie,
Argumentum testimonii est inartificiale.
To contradict which, I say *Ramus* shall dye.

(It is a bit like Book II, Chap. VI, in Rabelais, when Pantagruel met with a Limosin, who affected to speak in learned phrase: 'My friend, from whence comest thou now? The scholar answered him, from the *alme, inclyte* and celebrate academy, which is *vocitated Lutetia.* What is the meaning of this? said Pantagruel to one of his men.')

3.

Perhaps because this play has come down to us in so wretchedly garbled a version as to be but a skeleton of the thing Marlowe intended, those good passages in it seem somehow enhanced in our eyes, and his selection of images, his choice of action on the stage to make those images vivid, appear masterly. Witness the following:

> *Guise.* My Lord of Anioy, there are a hundred
> Protestants,
> Which we haue chaste into the riuer Sene,
> That swim about and so preserue their liues:
> How may we doe? I feare me they will liue.
> *Dumaine.* Goe place some men vpon the bridge,
> With bowes and dartes to shoot at them they see,
> And sinke them in the riuer as they swim.

Again, 'fiue or sixe Protestants with bookes' kneel on the stage in a huddle of terror. Guise enters with his murderous followers, and the scene is like a lightning flash upon an event fast fading into history. It is the poet's art of imagery transferred to the stage and there projected as drama. And because Marlowe knew that even the soul of a villain can be shaken, he brings his audience into the household of the Duke to strike at his heart and hearth:

> *Guise.* What, all alone my loue, and writing too:
> I prethee say to whome thou writest?
> *Duch.* To such a one my Lord, as when she reads
> My lines,
> Will laugh I feare me at their good aray.

But he feels the horns of the cuckold sprouting from his brow.

> *Guise.* I pray thee let me see.
> *Duch.* O no my Lord, a woman only must
> Partake the secrets of my heart.
> *Guise.* But Madam I must see.   *He takes it.*
> Are these your secrets that no man must know?
> *Duch.* O pardon me my Lord.

Thus is ambitious Guise characterized in life. His death sets the pattern for *Edward II*—and ultimately for Shakespeare:

> *Guise.* Villaine, why dost thou look so ghastly?
>   speake.
> *Mur.* O pardon me my Lord of Guise.
> *Guise.* Pardon thee, why what hast thou done?
> *Mur.* O my Lord, I am one of them that is set
>   to murder you.

Guise. To murder me villaine?

Mur. I my Lord, the rest haue taine their standings
in the next roome, therefore good my Lord goe
not foorth.

Guise. Yet *Caesar* shall goe forth.
Let mean consaits, and baser men feare death,
But they are pesants, *I* am Duke of *Guise:*
And princes with their lookes ingender feare.

Nevertheless, he is stabbed.

Now Henry exclaims (in Marlowe's patriotic vein, useful in settling an old score):

I nere was King of France vntill this houre:
This is the traitor that hath spent my golde
In making forraine warres and ciuil broiles.
Did he not draw a sorte of English priestes
From Doway to the Seminary at Remes,
To hatch forth treason gainst their naturall Queene?

Only Marlowe could have made a Catholic monarch
express such sentiments. He, too, could use religion as a
device of policy.

CHAPTER XV

Marlowe Dedicates a Book

I.

IN AUGUST, 1592, the plague broke out, closing the playhouses and sending the companies into the provinces. The following month Robert Greene died, and his death created as much of a stir as his miserable life, bringing the scandalmongers buzzing to his grave—and the protests of Marlowe and Shakespeare against his final impropriety.

In October, when the Michaelmas Sessions of the Peace were held, at which Marlowe was to appear on his recognizance, the poet failed to show up; at least, there is no record that he did. If he left London while the plague was raging, it would have been difficult to collect the twenty pounds for which he was liable as a result of his encounter with the constables. He carried his worldly possessions in his mind, on his back and in his pockets.

By November, his friend Watson also was dead, leaving for the press a book entitled *Amintae Gaudia*, and a request that it be dedicated to the Countess of Pembroke.

To this loving task Marlowe set himself, writing in Latin 'To the Most Illustrious Noble Lady, adorned with all gifts both of mind and body, Mary Countess of Pembroke.' As the only Dedication by him that has come down to us, it assumes a unique place in the canon of his works, and I give it here:

'Delia born of a laurel-crowned race, true sister of Sidney the bard of Apollo; fostering parent of letters, to whose immaculate embrace virtue, outraged by the assault of barbarism and ignorance, flieth for refuge, as once Philomela from the Thracian tyrant; Muse of the Poets of our time, and of all most happily burgeoning wits; descendant of the gods, who impartest now to my rude pen breathings of a lofty rage, whereby my poor self hath, methinks, power to surpass what my unripe talent is wont to bring forth: Deign to be patron to this posthumous Amyntas, as to thine adoptive son: the rather that his dying father had most humbly bequeathed to thee his keeping. And though thy glorious name is spread abroad not only among us but even among foreign nations, too far ever to be destroyed by the rusty antiquity of Time, or added to by the praise of mortals (for how can anything be greater than what is infinite?), yet, crowned as thou art by the songs of many as by a starry diadem Ariadne, scorn not this pure priest of Phoebus bestowing another star upon thy crown: but with that sincerity of mind which Jove the father of men and of gods hath linked as hereditary to thy noble family, receive and watch over him. So shall I, whose slender wealth is but the seashore myrtle of Venus, and Daphne's evergreen laurel, on the foremost page of every poem invoke thee as Mistress of the Muses to my aid: to sum up all, thy virtue, which shall overcome virtue herself, shall likewise overcome even eternity.

'Most desirous to do thee honor, C.M.' [1]

It is very learned and very pretty. Despite his fervent declaration, no poem of his invokes the Countess as 'Mistress of the Muses' or bears her name, although he might have dedicated *Hero and Leander* to her if he had lived; but he did insert a compliment to her in *Edward II*.

This was the lady whom the poets vied to honor with verse and dedication, the *Delia* of Samuel Daniel's sonnets, at whose death William Browne of Tavistock wrote his monumental praise:

> Underneath this sable herse
> Lies the subject of all verse:
> Sidney's sister, Pembroke's mother:
> Death, ere thou hast slain another
> Fair and learn'd and good as she,
> Time shall throw a dart at thee.

Aubrey described her thus: 'She was a beautiful Ladie and had an excellent witt, and had the best breeding that that age could afford. She had a pritty sharpe-ovall face. Her haire was of a reddish yellow.' What else he adds is scandalous, which gives Marlowe's praise of her virtue a sardonic sound.

2.

The death of Thomas Watson, the death of Greene, did not go unnoticed. The tribute of dramatic exequies was to be theirs—Thomas Nashe, the friend of both, saw to that. But the year that marked the breaking up of the writers' cluster was a plague year. The end of two literary men counted for nought in a city where thousands cowered behind bolted doors as the carts of the heaped dead wound pyreward through pestilent streets. The metropolis was beleaguered by death. 'Lord, have mercy upon us' was the salutation of citizens, the refrain of preachers. Terror took London.

From terror, courage; from horror, beauty. Past the hideous cowled skeleton and hooded skull, image of the plague, the vision of man's brief, bitter, earthbound destiny came to Nashe, in strayed music to haunt the meadow death had scythed:

> Beauty is but a flowre,
> Which wrinckles will deuoure,
> Brightnesse falls from the ayre,
> Queenes haue died yong and faire,
> Dust hath closde Helens eye.
> I am sick, I must dye:
> Lord, haue mercy on vs.

The poem is the jewel of *Svmmers Last Will and Testament*, the only dramatic work of Nashe's presumed many that has escaped the ravages of time, pestilence and fire. Completion of the play found him a pamphleteer again, and squirting Gabriel Harvey black with ink— *Have With Yov to Saffron-Walden* is his scoffing title.

In it he salutes Watson's memory: 'A man he was that I dearely lou'd and honor'd, and for all things hath left few his equalls in *England*—' and then the pattern of his prose reappears, praise for the friend and a sharp thrust at the foe: 'he it was that in the company of diuers Gentlemen one night at supper at the Nags head in *Cheape;* first told me of his vanitie, and those Hexameters made of him,

> *But o what newes of that good* Gabriell Haruey,
> *Knowne to the world for a foole and clapt in the Fleet*
>   *for a Rimer.'*

Despite the profusion of pronouns, it was clear enough in Nashe's context—particularly to Harvey, who later denied that he had ever been arrested; but this paid him back, in part, for his notions about versification, and for his temerity in mixing with professional writers. We can, of course, imagine Marlowe in similar settings, similar company, over supper in Cheapside taverns.

3.

As for Harvey himself, we are about to get news of him, for he is in the metropolis on business. Harvey is not easy to understand. It is strange to find him, a gentleman and Fellow of Pembroke Hall, Spenser's particular friend and the friend of courtiers, scholars and ecclesiastics, bandying words with the University wits in London. Barred from their society, the butt of their jokes and sarcasms for being a pedant and prig, Harvey nevertheless found his greatest delight in writing about them and forcing his presence on them—individually; it was prob-

ably risky to come upon them in a group. Those who know
the complexities of men may be able to explain this. The
pamphlet war in which he and Nashe suddenly engaged,
the attack of one being followed swiftly by the scurrilous,
racy prose counter-attack of the other, in violent strophe
and antistrophe, finally reached such a pitch of personal
vituperation that the authorities stepped in and ordered
'that all Nashe's bookes and Doctor Harvyes bookes be
taken wheresoeuer they maye be found.'

CHAPTER XVI

The Death of Greene

I.

A S ROBERT GREENE lay dying, sorrow for his
lost, misspent youth and life surged through him
like a fever. Weeping, he forgot the humble room—a
stranger's—he lay in, his once fine garments in tatters, his
wracked body ulcered by the Great Pox syphilis, his hair
unkempt, and the pointed red beard that had been his
pride knotted and foul with lice and London mud.

Like Villon before him in another land, he could
mourn the evil fortune that had overtaken him, contrast-
ing present, persistent ills with the days of brightness
that had been: 'Dear God! had I but heeded my books
in the days of my flaming youth, and given some thought
to good conduct, I might have had my own house, and
a soft bed to lie in! But Lord! I fled the Schoole like a
naughty child. As I write this my heart is like to break.'[1]
Thus Villon; and thus Greene presently. Gone are the
madcap fellows who kept him company—silent their jests
like their friendship. Gone are the giggling girls who
swarmed about him when his purse was full—silent their
satin-shrill voices, or cooing, but not for him, in another's
chamber, where gold lies on the table. A month before
there had been one wild burst of revelry—the last—and

then he had eaten and drunk himself into a stupor, feasting on pickled herring washed down by Rhine wine. He recalls it now—it is like a dream. Nashe had been there, the erstwhile disciple. It is over. Gone, too, now is the splendor of his promise, faded the glory of his achievements. He has reached the end of surfeiting in a shoemaker's house near Dowgate, by the river, half-starved and ragged, where he will die in loneliness. Therefore he weeps, and Death, stooping over his bed, peers down into a face grotesque with sorrow. A few discolored teeth, as the parched lip goes back, appear like withered ghosts writhing from a tomb.

All is gone: youth, health, life itself. Of his worldly store, of goods and precious time, nothing is left but a parcel of minutes—sand in the hourglass, sifting away. One final outpouring remains to him. He will set down his contrition on paper as a warning to others—ay, at the end, he will call upon his erstwhile companions, as loose and lecherous as himself, to give over a way of living that had brought him to such straits. In the room given him to die in, he calls for paper and pen, and feeling once more the old, familiar impulse of the makers, he sublimates his misery as he prepares his farewell to the world.

Now comes the cobbler's lady, who has some charity in her. She grants his last request—a penny pot of wine—and seeing the wild, unearthly stare in his red-rimmed eyes, backs out of Green's room, the antechamber of death, and tiptoes down to carry the news to her husband, who pauses in his cobbling, harks to all, and sighs, wondering, perhaps, if he will ever see again the money his strange lodger has cost him. For that is the way of the world.

Upstairs, wracked by suffering, an old hand at the writing game sets pen to paper: '*The Swan sings melodiously before death, that in all his life time vseth but a iarring sound.* Greene *though able inough to write, yet deeplyer serched with sickness than euer heeretofore, sendes you his Swanne like songe, for that he feares he shall neuer againe carroll to you wonted loue layes, neuer againe discouer to you youths pleasures.*'[2]

He sighs as though his very soul were issuing forth, for the words evoke memories, conjuring back from darkness and death the glory of youth and the high promise of his early fame. He has referred to a dozen lyrics, scattered through his works, which still delight by their simplicity and radiance—a handful of songs unsurpassed by any of his great contemporaries. For once again, in the strange annals of literature, a dissolute, riotous fellow has composed poems as lovely as love itself. And that, too, is the way of the world.

He pauses now, reads over what he has written, tasting to the full the pleasure of his well-rounded lines, knowing perhaps that never before has he written better. And so, in the proper mood at last, seizing the happy moments of authorship with zest in despite of death, he begins in earnest the composition of his *Groates-Worth of Witte, bought with a million of repentance,* sparing no detail of his detested course of living, and groveling lower and lower in a religious ecstasy, that he may be raised higher at the end.

If he forgets a scrap or two, it is no matter; he is reminded of others as he hears a scraping of feet at the door and turns to behold his mistress, who leads by the hand a shy, sickly boy, his bastard son, whom they have named Fortunatus. Small comfort they bring him; poverty has dogged them, too. Now they depart, and a bewildered boy looks backward from the door before he is gone forever.

His strength is ebbing, and he can scarcely write. But he is resolved, before he will stop, to send the warning he has conceived to his 'quondam acquaintances.' Marlowe heads the list, and him he addresses thus: 'Wonder not (for with thee wil I first begin) thou famous gracer of Tragedians, that *Greene*, who hath said with thee (like the foole in his heart) There is no God, shoulde now giue glorie vnto his greatness: for penetrating is his power, his hand lyes heauie vpon mee, hee hath spoken vnto mee with a voice of thunder, and I haue felt he is a God that can punish enemies.

'Why should thy excellent wit, his gift, bee so blinded, that thou shouldst giue no glorie to the giuer? Is it pestilent Machiuilian pollicy that thou hast studied? O peeuish follie!'

Time and illness have dimmed the scorn in his rival's lines:

To some perhaps my name is odious,
But such as loue me, gard me from their tongues,
And let them know that I am *Macheuill*,
And weigh not men, and therefore not mens words.

But as he points the moral—'The brocher of this Diabolicall Atheisme is dead, and in his life had neuer the felicitie hee aymed at'—he grows prophetic: 'Defer not (with me) till this last point of extremitie; for little knowst thou how in the end thou shalt be visited?'

2.

Now, with bitterness welling up anew in his wracked soul, he directs his attack toward one whose bright star was already in the ascendant: 'There is an vpstart Crow, beautified with our feathers, that with his *Tygers hart wrapt in a Players hyde*, supposes he is as well able to bombast out a blanke verse as the best of you: and being an absolute *Iohannes fac totum*, is in his owne conceit the onely Shake-scene in a countrey.'

It is the rising actor-playwright William Shakespeare on whose name he puns, as once he had punned on Marlowe's; and he twists with savage glee the line in *Henry VI*—'Oh tigers heart, wrapt'd in a woman's Hide'—that all may know who is meant.

Jealousy and rage drive the scratching pen across the paper, and he sighs as he comes to the end of his script and life itself. All is over for him; swiftly, swiftly, the sands of the hourglass sift downward, the candle burns down, the room is swarming with shadows.

Now, at the end, one ghost is at his side, and her familiar image walks the dark corridors of his mind: he hears the rustle of her skirt, recalls, as by a score of mirrors in whose midst she stands, the gestures, stride and attitude of his forsaken wife. Now, when self-pity might consume him, his thoughts enshrine her, converge on her, hold her snared; and though he has bought contrition with a million of repentance, he has another million, nay, more, to buy forgiveness at her hands. Once more he clutches the pen; he has said his farewell to the world—now he will take leave of her. The tears are hot now that were bitter before. He has come to the end that awaits all lonely men —the far-wanderers, the seekers after pleasure, the scoffers at custom and decorum, at order and the blessed humdrum of quiet lives. How blessed now, even in this miserable death, would be her presence, her hand upon his brow, her whispered words.

It is too late. His wild eyes glance around the room and see Death shuffling into a corner to wait his dying out.

How shall he begin? Addressing her, the pen lies useless in his hand; he is a mere novice at authorship, a schoolboy fearful and hesitant confronting a difficult theme; he is humble because of the image of her in his mind, the image of one he should have cherished but did not, to whom he had brought cares and had left in distress, whom he had upbraided when he should have succored: 'How often the Gentlewoman his Wife labored vainely to recall him, is lamentable to note: but as one giuen ouer to all his lewdnes, he communicated her sorrowful lines among his loose truls, that iested at her bootlesse laments.'

How shall he begin? 'The remembrance of many wrongs offered thee, and thy vnreprooued virtues, adde greater sorrow to my miserable state, then I can vtter, or thou conceiue.'

How plain the words seem, how insufficient, now that he has set them down. But it is a start: 'Neither is it lessened by consideration of thy absence (though shame would let me hardly beholde thy face) but exceedingly aggrauated, for that I cannot (as I ought) to thy owne selfe reconcile my selfe, that thou mightest witnesse my inward woe at this instant, that haue made thee a woeful wife for so long a time. But equal heauen hath denied that comfort, giuing at my last neede like succour as I haue sought all my life: being in this extremitie as voide of helpe, as thou hast beene of hope.

'Reason would, that after so long waste, I should not send thee a childe to bring thee greater charge; but consider, he is the fruit of thy wombe, in whose face regard not the fathers faults so much, as thy owne perfections. He is yet Greene, and may grow straight, if he be carefully tended: otherwise apt enough (I feare me) to follow his fathers folly.

'That I haue offended thee highly I knowe, that thou canst forget my iniuries I hardly beleeue: yet perswade I my selfe if thou saw my wretched state, thou couldest not but lament it: nay, certainely I knowe thou wouldest. Al my wrongs muster themselues about me, euery euill at once plagues me. For my contempt of God, I am contemned of men: for my swearing and forswearing, no man will beleeue me; for my gluttony, I suffer hunger: for my drunkennesse, thirst: for my adulterie, vlcerous sores.

'Thus God hath cast me downe, that I might be humbled: and punished me for example of others sinne: and although he suffers me in this world to perish without succour, yet trust I in the world to come to finde mercie, by the merits of my Sauiour, to whome I commend this, and commit my soule.

'Thy repentant husband for his disloyaltie. Robert Greene.'

Did ever man perish more miserably? None was at his bedside when he died, and only his hostess saw his body to the grave. His wife and child, and their subsequent struggles, fade from the knowledge of men.

CHAPTER XVII

A Puritan Confuted

I.

NOW comes Master Gabriel Harvey, ears sharp for literary gossip, 'to enquire after the famous Author: who was reported to lye dangerously sicke in a shoemakers house near Dow-gate: not of the plague, or the pockes, as a Gentleman saide, but of a surfett of pickle herringe and rennish wine.'

He threads his way through crowded streets to Dow-gate, and comes, not to a house of sickness, but to a house where death has called before him. It is September 5, 1592, a day after Greene's burial.

Harvey is well dressed; his manner is ingratiating. He confronts the simple woman of the house, sits at her table, and draws out her story, his retentive, spiteful memory noting all, cataloguing all, down to the cost of Greene's winding sheet, the charge of his interment. Eagerly she shows her visitor a note for ten pounds which Greene had bequeathed her husband, trusting perhaps that now it will be paid, that this fine gentleman so concerned over his dead friend—for such she supposes him to be—will square the account. Her eyes look hopefully on Harvey's face as he peers hard, memorizing the scrawl Greene has left behind, a doubtful legacy. The elves of satisfaction grimace and cavort in his mind. It is all as he could have wished. He bids the good woman adieu, with a bow—and is gone, secretly exulting. She remains speechless, clutching the note, and sees him disappear.

Now Harvey darts and dodges through Thames Street back to St. Paul's arriving at his publisher's establishment in a sweat, and promises to produce some additional and most delectable matter. He entitles his opus *Foure Letters, and certaine Sonnets: Especially touching Robert Greene* —the earlier pages have been overshadowed by his new material. He marshals fresh sheets of paper and seizes pen, feeling the gossip's urge to hound Greene in death who alive might have given him a drubbing for his pains. Yet something is due the deceased. Therefore he will rehearse the evil reputation of his victim, that what he has to add may be in order: 'Who in London hath not heard of his dissolute, and licentious liuing; his fonde disguisinge of a Master of Arte with ruffiantly haire, vnseemely apparell, and more vnseemelye Company: his vaineglorious and Thrasonicall brauinge: his piperly Extemporizing, and Tarletonizing; his apishe counterfeiting of euery ridiculous, and absurd toy: his fine coosening of Iugglers, and finer iuggling with cooseners; his villainous cogging, and foisting; his monstrous swearinge, and horrible forswearing; his impious profaning of sacred Textes: his other scandalous, and blasphemous rauinge: his riotous and outragious surfeitinge; his continuall shifting of lodgings: his plausible musteringe, and banquetinge of roysterly acquaintaunce at his first cominge; his beggarly departing in euery hostisses debt; his infamous resorting to the

Banckside, Shorditch, Southwarke, and other filthy
hauntes: his obscure lurkinge in basest corners: his pawn-
ing of his sword, cloake, and what not, when money came
short; his impudent pamphletting, phantasticall inter-
luding, and desperate libelling, when other coosening
shifts failed: his imployinge of Ball (surnamed Cuttinge
Ball) till he was intercepted at Tiborne, to leauy a crew of
his trustiest companions, to guarde him in daunger of
Arrestes: his keeping of the foresaid Balls sister, a sorry
ragged queane, of whome hee had his base sonne, *Infortunatus Greene:* his forsaking of his owne wife, too honest
for such a husband: particulars are infinite.'

He is but winded for a moment; he has put down
everything he could think of. He turns sanctimonious:
'They that haue seene much more than I haue heard: (for
so I am credibly infourmed) can relate straunge & almost
incredible Comedies of his monstrous disposition: where-
with I am not to infect the Aire, or defile this paper.'

It is a scholar, a courtier and a gentleman. Therefore
hark now to his account of his visit to the house near
Dowgate. Of his own imposture in drawing Greene's last
benefactor out, there is not a word: 'His hostisse *Isam* with
teares in her eies, & sighes from a deeper fountaine, (for
she loued him derely) tould me of his lamentable begging
of a penny pott of Malmesy: and, sir reurence how lowsy
he, and the mother of Infortunatus were (I would her
Surgeon found her no worse, then lowsey:) and how he
was faine poore soule, to borrow her husbandes shirte,
whiles his owne was a washing: and how his doublet, and
hose, and sword were sold for three shillinges: and besides

the charges of his winding sheete, which was foure shillinges; and the charges of hys buriall yesterday, in the
New-churchyard neere Bedlam, which was six shillinges,
and four pence; how deeply hee was indebted to her poor
husbande: as appeered by hys own bonde of tenne
poundes: which the good woman kindly showed me: and
beseeched me to read the writing beneath: which was a
letter to his abandoned wife, in the behalfe of his gentle
host: not so short as persuasible in the beginning, and pit-
tifull in the ending.

'*Doll, I charge thee by the loue of our youth, & by my
soules rest, that thou wilte see this man paide: for if hee,
and his wife had not succoured me, I had died in the
streetes.*'

How could Spenser put up with such a lout? one asks;
Nashe also raised the question: 'Immortall *Spencer*, no
frailtie hath thy fame, but the imputation of this Idiots
friendship.'

Thus died Greene, and thus did Harvey chronicle his
death. Fortunatus Greene, his bastard son, died the following year. Cutting Ball, brother of his mistress, was hanged
at Tyburn. Death and misfortune dogged them all.

2.

It was not to be supposed that Harvey's scurrilous
pamphlet would go unanswered, and the publication of
Foure Letters found Nashe in a mood to even the score.
In *Fovre Letters Confvted* he set forth his deceased

friend's virtues, and to make them more impressive he compared them with Harvey's lack of them. Greene had been 'a good fellowe'; he sees him in memory with his pointed red beard wagging, and nostalgia for past times in Cheapside taverns gives his prose a sad, quiet murmur. It is Nashe at his best, belaboring Harvey, defending Greene: 'Hee inherited more vertues than vices: a jolly long red peake, like the spire of a steeple, hee cherisht continually without cutting, whereat a man might hang a Iewell, it was so sharpe and pendant.

'Why should art answer for the infirmities of manners? Hee had his faultes, and thou thy follyes.

'Debt and deadly sinne, who is not subject to? with any notorious crime I neuer knew him tainted; (& yet tainting is no infamous surgerie for him that hath beene in so many hote skirmishes).'

So much for Greene's lechery. Did he drink, too? Why, what was money for? It was Greene's own money: 'A good fellowe hee was, and would haue drunke with thee for more *angels* then the Lord thou libeldst on *gaue thee in Christs Colledge;* and in one yeare he pist as much against the walls, as thou and thy two brothers spent in three.'

So much for Greene's tippling. He was a hard worker notwithstanding: 'In a night & a day would he haue yarkt vp a Pamphlet as well as in seuen yeare, and glad was that Printer that might bee so blest to pay him deare for the very dregs of his wit.

'Hee made no account of winning credite by his workes, as thou dost, that dost no good workes, but thinkes to bee famosed by a strong faith of thy owne worthines: his only

care was to haue a spel in his purse to coniure vp a good
cuppe of wine with at all times.'

Now Tom Nashe warms to his labors. The fine figure
of his friend, garbed in a great green cloak, with the sharp
red beard thrusting downward over it, strides through his
mind as he thumbs Harvey's malignant paragraphs. He
knows somewhat about Greene's apparel, and the sums
spent on it; and a thing or two about the last feast with
him on which Harvey has animadverted. Now, then,
'harke in your eare': 'For the lowsie circumstances of his
pourety before his death, and sending that miserable
writte to his wife, it cannot be but thou lyest, learned
Gabriell.

'I and one of my fellowes, *Will. Monox* (hast thou
neuer heard of him and his great dagger?) were in company with him a month before he died, at that fatall ban-
quet of Rhenish wine and pickled hearing (if thou wilt
needs haue it so), and then the inuentorie of his apparrell
came to more than three shillings (though thou saist the
contrarie). I know a Broker in a spruce leather ierkin with
a great number of golde Rings on his fingers, and a bunch
of keies at his girdle, shall giue you thirty shillings for the
doublet alone, if you can helpe him to it. Harke in your
eare, hee had a very faire Cloake with sleeues, of a graue
goose turd greene; it would serue you as fine as may bee;
No more words, if you bee wise, play the goodhusband
and listen after it, you may buy it ten shillings better
cheape than it cost him.'

And recalling Harvey's beginnings, his father a rope-
maker, and Harvey's friends at Court, he lays on a final

thwack and thump: 'By S. Siluer, it is good to bee circumspect in casting for the worlde, theres a great many ropes go to ten shillings. If you want a greasy paire of silk stockings also, to shew your selfe in at the Court, they are there to be had too amongst his moueables.'

About the matter of Greene's clothes, both Nashe and Harvey may have been in the right—one recalling what his friend had been wont to wear; the other learning what these had dwindled to as Greene stumbled from a pawnbroker's shop into the gutter, via the nearest tavern. Who Will Monox was I do not know—perhaps one that had drawn his dagger to affright Gabriel Harvey withal.

CHAPTER XVIII

Apology to Marlowe and Shakespeare

I.

TO Henry Chettle, playwright and printer, fell the task of seeing Greene's *Groates-Worth of Witte* licensed and printed. It proved embarrassing. To begin with, although he was a compositor, and had gazed dejectedly at many a writer's scrawl, this deathbed scribble of Greene's was perhaps the worst. The manuscript being in his care, he must perforce copy it for licensing. Copying another writer's work is tedious. Then there was the question of libel.

As he drove his pen on, supplying punctuation and paragraphing, as he was later to admit, he came upon a page that halted his hand between the inkhorn and paper and brought a furrow into his fat brow. A writer himself, he hesitated to take liberties with another's text. On the other hand, he had heard of Marlowe. He therefore left out a line or two—which blunted, he hoped, the sharpness of Greene's admonition. He had heard of Shakespeare also, and his high standing as a man and as a writer. Again he skipped in his copying. It was a secret and reverential mark of homage, spontaneous and honest. But it did not save him from trouble.

At the first perusals of Greene's pages a stir ran through

St. Paul's. The book fell like a pebble into the placid pond of the dead time of the year, and ripples, ever widening, spread over literary London. Friends and enemies alike of the dead author conned it eagerly, and then hurried like couriers with secret and exciting news to buzz into each other's ears. How Greene would have exulted to view this posthumous success!

Finally *A Groates-Worth of Witte* reached the circles in which Marlowe and Shakespeare moved. What happened then can only be surmised from the sequel. It sent Chettle scurrying back to the book he had ushered into the world. And at his heels, apparently, came demands for satisfaction.

He must have wished that he had never seen the damnable manuscript, which a bookseller had entrusted to his care. He recalled his pains over it, his copying, his running to and fro, the labors of recording and the labors of printing. Then his perturbation gave way to indignation. He had always dealt fairly with all, and he had not changed. So he rolled up his sleeves and prepared to give a lusty whack or two in his own behalf. But when he actually made his retort, it was more in sorrow than in anger, although something of the latter crept in. For that was the nature of the man.

The *apologia* for his connection with Greene's book appears in the preface to Chettle's *Kind-Harts Dreame* which he rushed to the press in December, 1592. It begins thus: '*About three moneths since died* M. Robert Greene, *leauing many papers in sundry Booke sellers hands, among other his Groats-worth of wit, in which a letter written to diuers play-makers, is offensiuely by one or two of them taken, and because on the dead they cannot be auenged, they wilfully forge in their conceites a liuing Author: and after tossing it two and fro, no remedy, but it must light on me.'*

There is no satisfaction in the dead, so a living culprit must be had—yet, wherefore me? he asks. Others may have forgotten his fair dealing, but he will remind them: *'How I haue all the time of my conuersing in printing hindred the bitter inueying against schollers, it hath been very well knowne, and how in that I dealt I can sufficiently prooue.'* As for the present complainants, he did not even know them—with a bow toward Marlowe: *'With neither of them that take offence was I acquainted, and with one of them I care not if I neuer be:*

'The other, whome at that time I did not so much spare, as since I wish I had, for that as I haue moderated the heate of liuing writers, and might haue vsde my owne discretion (especially in such a case) the Author beeing dead, that I did not, I am as sory, as if the original fault had beene my fault, because my selfe haue seene his demeanor no lesse ciuill than he exelent in the qualitie he professes:

'Besides, diuers of worship haue reported, his vprightnes of dealing, which argues his honesty, and his facetious grace in writting, that aprooues his Art.'

Chettle had seen Shakespeare plain, and this was his reputation in 1592, when he was twenty-eight years old. Whatever bitterness, secret and soul-consuming, was to fester in his heart later, fortune smiled upon him from the first—his star was ever in the ascendant, and opposite to Marlowe's.

To the latter Chettle returns for a parting comment, for he strove to be fair: '*For the first, whose learning I reuerence, and at the perusing of* Greenes *Booke, stroke out what then in conscience I thought he in some displeasure writ: or had it beene true, yet to publish it, was intollerable: him I would wish to vse me no worse than I deserue.*'

There remained only to explain just what his share in Greene's book was, for Chettle is nothing if not thorough, but even at the end his good thoughts for another break through, for he had heard, besides indignation, a few ugly rumors going the rounds: '*I had onely in the copy this share, it was il written, as sometimes* Greenes *hand was none of the best, licensd it must be, ere it could bee printed which could neuer be if it might not be read. To be breife I writ it ouer, and as neare as I could, followed the copy, onely in that letter I put something out, but in the whole booke not a worde in, for I protest it was all* Greenes, *not mine nor Maister* Nashes, *as some vniustly haue affirmed.*'

It has the ring of honesty. Nashe, defending himself against caluminators, conveniently forgot his alliance with Greene some years before: '*I neuer abusd Marloe, Greene, Chettle in my life, nor anie of my frends that vsde me like a frend.*'

So here was Marlowe, also at twenty-eight, with a reputation which a vicious individual could turn against him to his harm. Greene's ill-advised, ill-tempered lines, were barbed shafts that fell short of their mark, but before the end another drew the bow—a meaner, inferior but craftier enemy; not a writer.

At twenty-eight Marlowe had not yet learned to put a check on his tongue. He said what he pleased the moment a thought took form in his mind, and the words came tumbling forth to shock and astonish. He was not one to fret unduly over the effect; those who did not see things his way were dullards.

For the present he was safe. Chettle's apology was not all perhaps that he could have wished, but it was something. It gave notice, if notice were needed, that Christopher Marlowe would strike back as the occasion demanded. But against the hireling drawing up a secret indictment, against words wrung forth on the rack, the prisoner babbling to save himself, there would be no defense. His opinions had become doubly dangerous because he blurted them out to blabbers like himself.

Shakespeare he knew, but not, apparently, Polonius:

> Give thy thoughts no tongue,
> Nor any unproportion'd thought his act.
> Be thou familiar, but by no means vulgar;
> The friends thou hast, and their adoption tried,
> Grapple them to thy soul with hoops of steel;
> But do not dull thy palm with entertainment
> Of each new-hatch'd, unfledg'd comrade. Beware
> Of entrance to a quarrel, but, being in,
> Bear't that th' opposed may beware of thee.

He might have praised the writing, but its philosophy was not for him—save, perhaps, that part about a quarrel.

2.

Despite the gathering chorus of calumny, and the general acceptance of his character as reckless and unsteady, Marlowe in 1592, with less than a year of life remaining to him, was in the plentitude of his powers, renowned among the renowned. Writers—illustrious as some of them were—were not his only friends; and even in the attacks of his enemies or ill-wishers, respect for his achievements was writ large. He moved unperturbed from tavern table or bookseller's stall to the society of noblemen, for he had found it a simple matter, as he himself wrote, to

> cast the scholler off,
> And learne to court it like a Gentleman.

It was not only through the dedication of his friend Watson's posthumous book that Marlowe had access to the Countess of Pembroke's circle; his latest drama, *Edward II*, was now being 'sundrie times publiquely acted in the honourable citie of London, by the right honourable the Earle of Pembrooke his seruantes.' A compliment to the earl's wife, imbedded in that work, implies a greater familiarity with his lordship than the bare announcement on the title-page would indicate:

My house is not farre hence, out of the way
A little, but our men shall go along.
We that haue prettie wenches to our wiues,
Sir, must not come so neare and balke their lips.

It is spoken by an earlier Pembroke.

The end was at hand; the work was pouring forth. This is the play that shows how Marlowe, if he had lived, would have matured; this is the book with which Shakespeare went to school.[1] Only five years had elapsed since *Tamburlaine*, but there is here a development as impressive as Shakespeare's was to be—perhaps it was more impressive, for at this time, Shakespeare, the same age as Marlowe, had not produced anything to compare with this tragedy; it was many years before he did.

For the story of Edward and his favorite, Gaveston, and the revolt of the nobles against their sinister friendship, Marlowe turned to Holinshed's *Chronicle*. The bare bones were there. But the perfections of *Edward II* emerge within the framework of a wholly realized art form—perhaps here, for the first time in his life as a writer for the stage, Marlowe was master of his medium: skilled in motivation, sure in development of character. Queen Isabel is a woman, scorned by Edward, loved by Mortimer, tragic and passionate, but never the dim, idealized vision beheld by Tamburlaine or Faustus. Ambition drives Mortimer within grasp of the throne, and weakness and disease of the spirit drag Edward down to abdication and death at the hands of hirelings. Marlowe had observed, with becoming cynicism, the ways of the fine-furred world:

The troublesome

raigne and lamentable death of
Edward *the second, King of*
England : with the tragicall
fall of proud Mortimer:

As it was fundrie times publiquely acted
in the honourable citie of London, by the
right honourable the Earle of Pem-
brooke his seruants.
Written by Chri. Marlow *Gent.*

Imprinted at London for. *William Iones,*
dwelling neere Holbourne conduit at the
signe of the Gunne, 1594

Tis not a black coate and a little band,
A Veluet cap'de cloake, fac'st before with Serge,
And smelling to a Nosegay all the day,
Or holding of a napkin in your hand,
Or saying a long grace at a tables end,
Or making lowe legs to a noble man,
Or looking downeward with your eye lids close,
And saying, trulie ant may please your honor,
Can get you any fauour with great men,
You must be proud, bold, pleasant, resolute,
And now and then, stab as occasion serues.

Much that Shakespeare was to do is found in *Edward II* in epitome, and all of it is shadowed forth in verse not even he surpassed—the steady revelation of great spirits in opposition, like planets tugging in their orbits; the searching soliloquy, and the close-packed, intense lines. Rash and intemperate Marlowe may have appeared to some, but on the evidence of this play something serene and deeply felt in him was gathering into beauty for a second harvest.

It is the death scene of Marlowe's king:

These lookes of thine can harbor nought but death.
I see my tragedie written in thy browes,
Yet stay a while, forbeare thy bloudie hande,
And let me see the stroke before it comes,
That euen then when I shall lose my life,
My minde may be more stedfast on my God.

What meanes your highnesse to mistrust me thus?

What meanes thou to dissemble with me thus?

These handes were neuer stainde with innocent bloud,
Nor shall they now be tainted with a kings.

Forgiue my thought, for hauing such a thought,
One iewell haue I left, receiue thou this.
Still feare I, and I know not whats the cause,
But euerie iointe shakes as I giue it thee:
O if thou harborst murther in thy hart,
Let this gift change thy minde, and saue thy soule,
Know that I am a king, oh at that name
I feele a hell of greefe: where is my crowne?
Gone, gone, and doe I remaine aliue?

Your ouerwatchde my lord, lie downe and rest.

But that greefe keepes me waking, I shoulde sleepe,
For not these ten daies haue these eyes lids closd.
Now as I speake they fall, and yet with feare
Open againe. O wherefore sits thou heare?

If you mistrust me, ile be gon my lord.

No, no, for if thou meanst to murther me,
Thou wilt returne againe, and therefore stay.

He sleepes.

O let me not die yet, stay, O stay a while.

How now my Lorde.

Something still busseth in mine eares,
And tels me, if I sleepe I neuer wake,
This feare is that which makes me tremble thus,
And therefore tell me, wherefore art thou come?

To rid thee of thy life.

Thus, in pity and terror, the climax of the play comes, and the great characters that people it turn shadowward. In the Earl of Mortimer who led the nobles against their sovereign, Marlowe has again projected an aspiring protagonist, but this one is a man, motivated by hatred of Gaveston and love of country and his queen, a tragic figure who nurses his own doom in safeguarding Edward's son. He meets death like an Elizabethan, with a sublime utterance whose echoes we hear in *Julius Caesar* and *Hamlet:*

Base fortune, now I see, that in thy wheele
There is a point, to which when men aspire,
They tumble hedlong downe: that pointe I touchte,
And seeing there was no place to mount vp higher,
Why should I greeue at my declining fall?
Farewell faire Queene, weepe not for *Mortimer,*
That scornes the world, and as a traueller,
Goes to discouer countries yet vnknowne.

CHAPTER XIX

Depression and a Play

I.

NATIONALISM is the child of economics, fathered anew by every lean age. Witness an incident three and a half centuries ago. It is London, in the spring of 1593. In streets where the aliens dwell there are murmuring, menacing groups, a sudden barrage of stones against barred and bolted doors; burly apprentices roar past the huddle of houses, bellowing for combat. The men of the watch come running with a heavy-footed clatter, and the cry rises: 'prentices and clubs,' to beat the officers down.

The scene shifts to the House of Commons. A new bill, 'against Alien Strangers selling by way of Retail any Foreign Commodities,' is up for discussion.[1]

Sir John Wolley: 'This Bill should be ill for *London*, for the Riches and Renown of the City cometh by entertaining of Strangers, and giving liberty unto them.'

Mr. Fuller: 'The exclamations of the City are exceeding pitiful and great against these Strangers; nay had not these latter quiet times in their own Countries, and our troubles made many of them retire home, the Citizens would have been in uproar against them: The which if the Government of the City repress not, they will be apt enough to it.'

Mr. Finch: 'We ought not to be uncharitable, but this must be the Rule. None must so relieve Strangers, as by it to beggar themselves. But for their riches, it groweth chiefly by Parsimony, and where they dwell I see not the Nation is so much grieved at them as here in *London*, for they contribute to all Scots and Lots as we do. Though they be a church by themselves, their Example is profitable amongst us, for their Children are no sooner able to go, but they are taught to serve God, and to flee idleness; for the least of them earneth his meat by his labour. Our Nation is sure more blessed for their sakes. Wherefore as the Scripture saith, *Let us not grieve the Soul of the stranger.*'

Sir Walter Raleigh (member for Devonshire): 'Whereas it is presented, that for Strangers it is against Charity, against Honour, against profit to expel them; in my opinion it is no matter of *Charity* to relieve them. For first, such as fly hither have forsaken their own King, and Religion is no pretext for them, for we have no Dutchmen here, but such as came from those Princes where the Gospel is Preached, and here they live disliking our Church. For *Honour*, It is Honour to use Strangers as we be used amongst Strangers; And it is a lightness in a Common-Wealth, yea a baseness in a Nation to give a liberty to another Nation which we cannot receive again. In *Antwerp* where our intercourse was most, we were never suffered to have a Taylor or a Shoemaker to dwell there. Nay at *Millain* where there are three hundred pound English men, they cannot have so much as a Barber amongst them. And for *Profit*, they are all of the House of *Almoigne,* who pay nothing, yet eat out our profits, and supplant our own Nation. Custom indeed they pay, paying fifteen pence where we pay twelve pence, but they are discharged of Subsidies.'

The voices of the honorable members rise to a drone. Twenty-five years later, on Tower Hill, Sir Walter, what thought you of charity then? A scarce commodity, was it not, O wanderer over the world!

So thought the French and Flemings, parsimonious weavers and tradesmen flourishing in an alien land, who had watched their families grow with their hoards, and whose eyes and ears now sentineled their households in the troubled days and nights. So thought the prosperous Dutch, cloth merchants to the world, whose tidy souls gave prayers and praise to God in their own church in Austin Friars, which Edward VI had granted them to be an orthodox rampart in the troubled sea of London. In the streets of the aliens inexplicable fear seizes the children as they watch bolts and bars clatter into place, and hear, beyond the door and window, the hostile murmur.

2.

In the tense city, a group of writers met to talk over a play.[2] Their protagonist was Sir Thomas More who, as Sheriff of London under Henry VIII, had faced an apprentices' uprising against foreigners during a depression year. London would flock to see current events depicted in historical guise, with all the braveries of verse to stir the English heart:

My searching eye did neuer entertaine
A more distracted countenaunce of greefe
Then I haue late obseru'de
In the displeased commons of the cittie.

That was for the unemployed 'prentices and their wives, and their masters and masters' wives, too. Out of their discontent the tocsin beat:

But if the Englishe blood be once but vp,
As I perceiue theire harts alreadie full
I feare me much, before their spleenes be coolde,
Some of these saucie aliens for their pride
Will pay for't soundly, wheresoere it lights—

beat until it became reckless and an incitement to rebellion:

Then gallant bloods you whoes fre sowles doo skorne
To beare the inforsed wrongs of aliens
Ad rage to ressolutione fier the howses
Of theis audatious strangers.

The script or 'booke' of the play was submitted to Sir Edmund Tyllney, Master of the Revels, for licensing; it came back, license refused. In the margin at the top of the first sheet of dialogue the astonished collaborators read the following threatening memorandum: 'Leaue out the insurrection wholy & the Cause theroff & begin with Sir Tho: Moore att the mayors sessions with a report afterwards off his good service done being Shrieve off London vppon a mutiny Agaynst the Lumbards only by A shortt reportt & nott otherwise att your own perilles.' [3]

Hastily thumbing through their manuscript, they saw repeated objections to the word 'strangers,' a marginal note, 'Mend this,' whole scenes crossed out. To save the play, a new writer was called in, whose contribution was a revised insurrection scene. Was it Marlowe or Shakespeare? The humanity of Shakespeare is apparent in More's address to the insurgents:

> Go you to Fraunce or Flanders,
> To any Jarman prouince, to Spaine or Portigall,
> Nay, any where that not adheres to Ingland,—
> Why, you must needes be straingers: woold you be
>   pleasd
> To find a nation of such barbarous temper,
> That, breaking out in hiddious violence,
> Would not afoord you an abode on earth—?

There is no record to show that the play was ever produced. But from subsequent events, it appears that Sir Edmund Tyllney had not only exercised his prerogative of official censor, but had submitted the names of the authors to the Privy Council.

One of them was Thomas Kyd.

3.

The final phase of the drama opens against a background of demoralizing plague, with church bells tolling gloom. There appeared, suddenly, on walls and doors, printed manifestoes threatening the 'strangers' if they did not forthwith leave the city. One of them was the wall of the Dutch church in Austin Friars. Admonished by resident ambassadors, Her Majesty's Privy Council prodded the Lord Mayor, and several brawlers were seized, put into stocks, carted about and whipped at crossroads. Then, in desperation, at a Star Chamber meeting on May 11, the Council lashed out. Present were Whitgift, the Lord Archbishop; Sir John Puckering, Lord Keeper of the Great Seal and Her Majesty's Chancellor; Burghley, the Lord Treasurer; the Earl of Derby; Lord Buckhurst, onetime gentleman author; Sir John Fortescue, and Sir Robert Cecil, Elizabeth's 'little man,' now grooming himself to take his father's place: 'A letter to Sir Richard Martin, Anthonie Ashley, Mr. Alderman Buckle, &c.: [4]

'There haue bin of late diuers lewd and mutinous libells set up within the citie of London, among the which there is some set uppon the wal of the Dutch Churchyard that doth exceed the rest in lewdness, and for the discouerie of the author and publisher thereof hir Maiesties pleasure is that some extraordinarie paines and care be taken by you commissioners appointed by the Lord Maior for th' examining such persons as maie be in this case anie way suspected. Theis shalbe therefore to require and aucthorize you to make search and apprehend euerie person so to be suspected, and for that purpoze to enter into al houses and places where anie such maie be remayning. And, uppon their apprehencion, to make like search in anie the chambers, studies, chestes, or other like places for al manner of writings or papers that may geue you light for the discouerie of the libellers.'

It is but indifferent spelling and composition, but their Lordships have managed to convey the hysteria brought by them into the Star Chamber: 'And after you shall haue examined the persons, if you shal finde them dulie to be suspected, and they shal refuze to confesse the truth, you shal by aucthoritie hereof put them to the Torture in Bridewel, and by th' extremitie thereof, to be used at such times and as often as you shal think fit, draw them to discouer their knowledge concerning the said libells.'

The scribe, bent over his scratching quill, raises his head at the word 'torture,' and the thrust of steel in the speaker's voice earns a capital letter.

The letter is dispatched to the Lord Mayor's commissioners. Their Lordships fill the room with coughing, metamorphosed back into men. Informers swarm forth. The tragedy of Kyd and Marlowe swells to its fateful climax.

CHAPTER XX

The Arrest of Kyd

I.

THE stairs creak, there is a sound of tramping feet, and armed forms shuffling in the dark. A moment later a heavy hand smites loudly, authoritatively, on the door of Thomas Kyd's chamber, and a startled and perplexed author hastens to give his unexpected visitors entry.

It is the last free and uncompelled action of his life. Fate has marked *finis* to his career and hovers in the shadows with the law's minions.

Gruffly, a bailiff demands his 'papers.' Kyd points, like an automaton, to his table. He is bewildered, then terrified, as silence meets his questions and he sees the bailiff taking up his manuscripts. Passages merge and blur in his mind. The hard-breathing officer glances superciliously at the titles of volumes huddled together, then begins to pry into chests and drawers. The room is oppressive with men's breathing.

Patiently, with the patience of the slow-footed law, the bailiff examines each scrap of his new finds; patiently his men stand at their posts, shifting their wearisome positions or clearing fog-filled throats with forced, explosive coughs; and patiently, but not stolidly like the others, feeling his misgivings grow, Kyd eyes the movements of the prober, and starts as the bailiff straightens up, holding several pieces of paper to the light.

What has he found?

As one in a dream pursued by horrifying, sinister shapes, Kyd sees the men of the law close in about him. From oppressive warmth the room suddenly has turned cold, and an ague of fright holds him rooted to the spot. Then he is swept out of the room, in the midst of his heavy-footed abductors, down the stairs and into the fog-haunted street. He is under arrest. He is a prisoner. It is unreal. But now the wheels of his brain begin to whir and plunge. He trudges along, his mind full of projects for his swift release. In the streets he is leaving behind, wisps and strays of fog haunt the air.

2.

There was a great deal of mysterious bustle where he next found himself. The humorless ceremonies of the law chilled his soul, and it was not long before the glimmers of his confidence went out in terror before hostile authority. He was in Bridewell, the prey of inquisitors.

To a question about 'the booke of Sir Thomas More,' he replies that he is a playwright, not an inciter to rebellion.

To a question about the outbreaks against the aliens, he replies that he is not a masterless man, and not a brawler.

Then his tormentors let him be. He found himself alone, and experiencing that enormous loneliness com-

bined with helplessness which comes to all who are suddenly taken out of the teeming world to prison. All
through the night he heard loud voices and cries, and the
comings and goings of many men. Sleep at length pre-
vailed over the host of lugubrious thoughts that thronged
his brain. Under a roof that covered nightmares his tired
body had ease. He was beyond the cruelties of men for a
brief time.

Interrogations were resumed the next day. Suddenly
they ceased, and he was escorted to a room whose designa-
tion was awesome even to his jailors. He saw the rack, and
steeled himself for the ordeal. Between gasps, hands
clenched and teeth grinding hard, he continued to assert
his innocence and to beg that word be sent to his Lord.
It was then that he was shown three sheets of paper
seized, days ago, ages ago, in the chamber which was now
like a chamber in a dream, far off, full of peace and quiet,
where he had once lived.

The blood rushes to his face, speech vanishes from his
mind as he reads the terrifying notation on one of the
pages:

12 may 1593
vile hereticall Conceiptes
denyinge the deity of Jhesus
Christ our Savior fownd
emongest the papers of Thos
kydd prisoner.[1]

Kyd, at bay, looks up into a circle of death's head smiles.
He tries to explain. The papers had become 'shuffled'

with his own while sharing his room with another man, another writer.

Who is the man?

Again Kyd replies, and this time one of his examiners takes up a pen, dips it into an ink-pot, and writes under the earlier notation:

> which he affirmethe that he
> had ffrom Marlowe.

The commissioners scent new quarry, and look kindlier now upon their victim, who hangs abjectly, bruised and bloodied, a scarecrow of a man with gleams of terror for eyes.

It is May 18. Their findings are communicated to the Privy Council. An agent slips away from London to run the quarry down. He is Henry Maunder, one of the messengers of Her Majesty's Chamber, who has been ordered to 'repaire to the house of Mr. Tho: Walsingham in Kent, or to anie other place where he shall vnderstand Christofer Marlow to be remayning, and by virtue hereof to apprehend and bring him to the Court.' Their Lordships somewhat know their man, and they have added this laconic phrase: 'and in case of need to require ayd.' [2]

18 May 1593: the Privy Council sends for Marlowe.

20 May: 'commaunded to giue his daily attendaunce.'

CHAPTER XXI

Eros and Other Gods

I.

WHAT was it, in that somber spring, that turned the mind of Marlowe to love, the god toward whom no man is atheist? For, in the house of Mr. Thomas Walsingham in Kent, with less than two weeks of life remaining to him, he is writing a love poem in narrative form, of 'Hero the faire,' and 'Amorous *Leander*, beautifull and yoong.' We know him so well and so little! What is imbedded in that line of his—

Who euer lov'd, that lov'd not at first sight?

and its reiteration—

True loue is mute, and oft amazed stands;

and the triumphant finale:

Treason was in her thought,
And cunningly to yeeld her selfe she sought.
Seeming not woon, yet woon she was at length,
In such warres women vse but halfe their strength.
Leander now like Theban *Hercules*,
Entred the orchard of *Th'esperides*,

Whose fruit none rightly can describe but hee
That puls or shakes it from the golden tree:
And now she wisht this night were neuer done,
And sigh'd to thinke vpon th' approaching sunne,
For much it greeu'd her that the bright day-light
Should know the pleasure of this blessed night,
And them like *Mars* and *Ericine* display,
Both in each others armes chaind as they lay.
Againe she knew not how to frame her looke,
Or speake to him who in a moment tooke
That which so long so charily she kept,
And faine by stealth away she would haue crept,
And to some corner secretly haue gone,
Leauing *Leander* in the bed alone.
But as her naked feet were whipping out,
He on the suddaine cling'd her so about,
That Meremaid-like vnto the floore she slid,
One halfe appear'd, the other halfe was hid.
Thus neere the bed she blushing stood vpright,
And from her countenance behold ye might
A kind of twilight breake, which through the heare,
As from an orient cloud, glymse here and there.
And round about the chamber this false morne
Brought foorth the day before the day was borne.

This much is certain: by love, or by as subtle a meta-
morphosis of the spirit, he had become once more the
youth of Corpus Christi, steeped in Ovid, wearing out
the hours in rhymed measures. And with his life turning
backward upon itself, the wheel of fortune turned.

2.

For now comes Master Maunder to Scadbury, asking discreetly if one Marlowe is there; he would have a word with him. He steps aside with the poet and communicates his tidings. A conference follows, and Marlowe is advised to present himself promptly to the Privy Council. He bids Thomas Walsingham and his lady adieu, and rides off to London, the lines of his poem ringing fainter and fainter in his mind.

There is a hush in the streets when he arrives; church bells, treading the air throughout London, send forth their peals, mingling their myriad-toned music in an anthem for the plague's dead. He comes to the shadowy buildings of government at Westminster, enters one, and is instantly enmeshed in the law's coils.

'I am Christopher Marlowe,' he announces.

A crafty, medieval face looks up into his. There is a rustle of paper as his *dossier* is run down; he waits, impatience gnawing the particles of his mind. He is admitted, at length, into the hushed presence of the ministers of state. His aspect is grave, to match the faces he sees there. He learns of Kyd's imprisonment with serious mien, and gives, in return, an account of their friendship—if it can be called that. Then he is shown the three sheets of paper Kyd has ascribed to him. He asks leave to peruse them, sees the notation—'vile hereticall Conceiptes,' etc.

He begins to read, his mind busy formulating a defense. He sees before him, written in a neat, clerkly,

Italian script, the ancient Arian heresy denying the divine origin of Jesus; twelve centuries before it had shaken Christendom, ushering in the confession of faith known as the Nicene creed. He reads: 'It is lawfull by many wayes to se the infirmitie of Jhesus Christ whom Paul in the last chapter to the Corinthians of the second Epistle denieth not to be crucified through infirmitie. And the whole course & consent of the Euangelicall history doth make him subject to the passions of man as hunger thirst wearines & fear. To the same end ar swete anxietie continuall praier the consolation of the Angell again spitting whipping rebukes or checks His corps wrapt in the linnen cloth vnburied And to beleue forsooth that this nature subiect to theis infirmities & passions is God or any part of the diuine essence what is it other but to make God mightie & of power of thone part weak & impotent of thother part which thing to think it wer madness & follie To persuade others impieties.'

It was a moment of mortal danger. This is precisely what killed Francis Kett, like Marlowe late of Corpus Christi, who died at the stake screaming before his life flickered and went out: 'Blessed be none but God.'

3.

The moment passed. Perhaps Marlowe looked up with a chuckle calculated to disarm and, handing over the sheets, named their source. For the three pages are merely a transcript from a book, *The Fal of the late Arrian*, printed in 1549, in which an antitrinitarian tract is quoted

Marlowe Baptized

'the 26th day of ffebruary' 1564

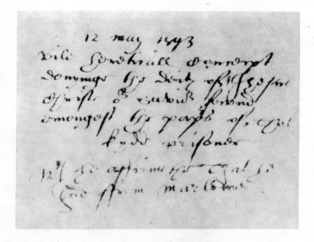

Marlowe In Trouble

'vile hereticall conceiptes'

Marlowe Buried

'1 of June' 1593: *'slaine'*

for purposes of confutation. (Whoever the unknown Socinian was, he had come into conflict with the Privy Council in the reign of Henry VIII, just as Kyd and Marlowe and others were to do in the reign of Henry's daughter.[1] The political and religious pattern is one of repetitions.) If Marlowe was asked how he knew this, he could have reminded his examiners that he had been a student of divinity.

As for the clerkly, Italian script found in the copy, it was not his handwriting; perhaps Kyd's—Marlowe's last sardonic jest at the expense of his friend. Who knows the heart of man?

Whatever his explanation was, it was decided that his being at large would not endanger the realm, for a Privy Council minute reveals he was not held: '20 May. This day Christofer Marley of London, gent., being sent for by warrant from their Lordships, hath entered his appearance accordinglie for his indemnity therein, and is commaunded to giue his daily attendaunce on their Lordships vntill he shall be licensed to the contrarie.'[2]

Had he been imprisoned, how different the story of his life and accomplishments might have been, for ten days later he was dead, at the age of twenty-nine.

Kyd, meanwhile, languished in Bridewell.

CHAPTER XXII

Marlowe's Table Talk (Continued)

I.

FOR Elizabeth's subjects the borderland between the spiritual and temporal realms lay in perpetual dusk, guarded by terrors, lit by leaping fires; no man might come upon it in his quest, and not be lost for his pains. The Tower and keeps of the city were not the sole buffers for the shock of rebellion; churches made arsenals in every parish, for orthodoxy meant obedience to the state as well as fear of the Lord. That is why, in the chambers of the Privy Council, the voice of Archbishop Whitgift rose, occasionally, higher than the voice of Her Majesty's Principal Secretary, now Sir John Puckering.

Under a lowering sky, under the dark and gabled houses whispering together, past shadowy doorways and noisy shops and taverns, a pious informer, one Richard Baines, picks his way to Westminster. Befitting a man who is bringing tidings to trouble another, he comes with exalted mien and tread. A rich garner is his—a collection of Marlowe's blasphemous utterances, fit to make the righteous rage. Baines rages as he begins: 'A note Containing the opinion of on(e) Christopher Marly Concerning his damnable Judgment of Religion, and scorn of Gods word.' [1]

194

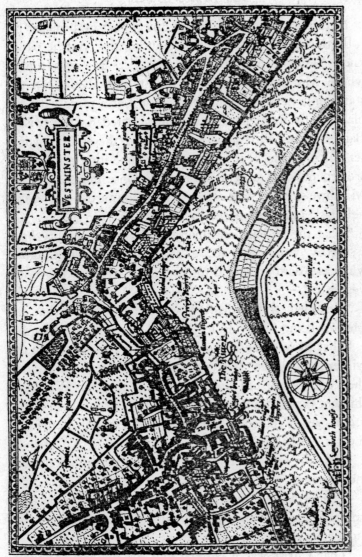

Elizabeth's Westminster

Nothing is known of Baines except that he brought his collection of Marlowiana to the authorities. But he either knew Marlowe himself, or he moved as an eavesdropper where Marlowe was known and talked about, for the statements he ascribes to the poet are of a piece with the blabbing by Kyd; perhaps he interrogated Kyd in prison. Baines writes with passion; here and there, first words set down in the heat and zeal of composition are merely crossed out and others substituted. Once more, we have Marlowe's table talk—from 1587 onwards—set down helter-skelter as gathered by Baines:

'That the Jndians and many Authors of antiquity haue assuredly writen of aboue 16 thowsand yeares agone whereas Adam is proued to haue lived within 6 thowsand yeares.

'He affirmeth that Moyses was but a Jugler & that one Heriots being Sir W Raleighs man Can do more then he.

'That Moyses made the Jewes to travell xl yeares in the wildernes, (which Jorney might haue bin done in lesse then one yeare) ere they Came to the promised land to thintent that those who were privy to most of his subtilties might perish and so an everlasting superstition Remain in the hartes of the people.

'That the first beginning of Religioun was only to keep men in awe.

'That it was an easy matter for Moyses being brought vp in all the artes of the Egiptians to abuse the Jewes being a rude & grosse people.

'That Christ was a bastard and his mother dishonest.

'That he was the sonne of a Carpenter, and that if the

Jewes among whome he was borne did Crucify him theie best knew him and whence he Came.

'That Christ deserved better to dy then Barrabas and that the Jewes made a good Choise, though Barrabas were both a thief and a murtherer.

'That if there be any god or any good Religion, then it is in the papistes because the service of god is performed with more Cerimonies, as Elevation of the mass, organs, singing men, Shaven Crownes & cta. That all protestantes are Hypocriticall asses.

'That if he were put to write a new Religion, he would vndertake both a more Exellent and Admirable methode and that all the new testament is filthily written.

'That the woman of Samaria & her sister were whores & that Christ knew them dishonestly.

'That St John the Evangelist was bedfellow to Christ and leaned alwaies in his bosome, that he vsed him as the sinners of Sodoma.

'That all they that loue not Tobacco & Boies were fooles.

'That all the apostles were fishermen and base fellowes neyther of wit nor worth, that Paull only had wit but he was a timerous fellow in bidding men to be subiect to magistrates against his Conscience.

'That he had as good Right to Coine as the Queen of England, and that he was acquainted with one Poole a prisoner in Newgate who hath greate Skill in mixture of mettals and hauing learned some thinges of him he ment through help of a Cunninge stamp maker to Coin ffrench Crownes pistoletes and English shillinges.

'That if Christ would haue instituted the sacrament with more Ceremoniall Reverence it would haue bin had in more admiration, that it would haue bin much better being administred in a Tobacco pipe.

'That the Angell Gabriell was baud to the holy ghost, because he brought the salutation to Mary.

'That on(e) Ric Cholmley hath Confessed that he was perswaded by Marloe's Reasons to become an Atheist.'

Behind Marlowe's callous and jolting quips—some of them mere tavern jests for a laugh from his fellows—there rings a skeptical mind courageously arrayed against the superstition and abuse which are the ancient and evidently inalienable allies of religion. That it was a dangerous sport, Baines's fulminating summation shows: 'These thinges, with many other shall by good & honest witnes be aproved to be his opinions and Comon Speeches and that this Marlow doth not only hould them himself, but almost into every Company he Cometh he perswades men to Atheism willing them not to be afeard of bugbeares and hobgoblins, and vtterly scorning both god and his ministers as J Richard Baines will Justify & approue both by mine oth and the testimony of many honest men, and almost al men with whome he hath Conversed any time will testify the same, and as J think all men in Christianity ought to indevor that the mouth of so dangerous a member may be stopped, he saith likewise that he hath quoted a number of Contrarieties oute of the Scripture which he hath giuen to some great men who in Convenient time shalbe named. When these thinges shalbe Called in question the witnes shalbe produced.' [2]

Righteous anger has clouded Baines's prose; his last
personal pronoun may refer to Cholmley or Kyd, but it
may also refer to Marlowe. This much is clear—Marlowe's reckless quips, apparently tossed off in any and all
company during his life in London, had reached a cumula-
tive climax which involved others who now stood in peril
from him.

2.

The informer had referred to 'some great men who in
Convenient time shalbe named.' He also offered to produce witnesses. This is intriguing, in view of immediate
and subsequent happenings.

A copy of the 'Note' was made for the perusal of Queen
Elizabeth. It was endorsed:

> Copye of Marloes
> blasphemyes.
> As sent to her *Highness*.[3]

It was not sent posthaste, however.

Two items concern us here—an omission and an addition in Baines's text. The phrase, 'being Sir W Raleighs
man' no longer appears; while in the margin of the paragraph about Cholmley, Marlowe's atheist convert, are the
words, 'he is layd for.'

There is a sinister conjunction here; much could be
made of it.

Cholmley had been in government service. A double-dealer at heart, he had finally rebelled against his employers. In 'Remembraunces of wordes and matter against Richard Cholmeley',[4] on file with the authorities, it was written: 'he speaketh in generall all euil of the Counsell,' and that 'being imployed by some of her Maiesties prevy Counsaile for the apprehension of Papistes, and other daungerous men, hee vsed, as he saieth, to take money of them and would let them pass in spighte of the Counsell.' The same paper reveals: 'hee saieth & verely beleueth that one Marlowe is able to shewe more sounde reasons for Atheisme then any devine in Englande is able to geue to prove devinitie & that Marloe tolde him that hee hath read the Atheist lecture to Sᵣ Walter Raliegh & others.'

What Marlowe's atheist lecture was there is no way of learning; perhaps the 'Contrarieties oute of the Scripture' cited by Baines. Cholmley obviously was acquainted with Marlowe; under what circumstances, we can only conjecture. But, as usual, the poet had talked recklessly. Baines had barely linked him to Raleigh, through his 'man' Harriot. Cholmley left nothing to inference. But was it not Raleigh and his friends whom Baines meant in that threatening reference to 'some great men who in Convenient time shalbe named'? And if his declaration concerning Marlowe, that 'all men in Christianity ought to indevor that the mouth of so dangerous a member may be stopped,' was an incitement to murder, as some writers believe, to whom would it have appealed?

Kyd was in prison, and talking about Marlowe's atheism and Marlowe's associates. Baines and Cholmley corroborated Kyd. What might not Marlowe himself reveal if newly examined—on the rack, for example, like Kyd?

These might have been matters for Raleigh to ponder.[5] At what would he have stopped to ward off peril to himself? 'If ever man drew vertue out of necessity, it was he.'[6] In a poem of great strength and great bitterness he even had written that homicide was justifiable:

> Because to giue the lie,
>   deserues no lesse than stabbing.

As their Lordships of the Privy Council still hesitated over the copy of Baines's report, deferred in the sending, Marlowe lay dead, stabbed in the head by a dagger. With this news, a Council scribe crossed out the heading and wrote in its place: 'A Note deliuered on Whitsun eve last of the most horrible blasphemes vtteryd by Christofer Marly who within iii dayes after came to a soden and fearfull end of his life.'[7]

CHAPTER XXIII

The Death of Marlowe

I.

IT IS Wednesday evening, May 30, 1593.
In a room of Eleanor Bull's tavern in Deptford, across the Thames from London, there are assembled four men who, after a day of talking and drinking, are 'in quiet sort together.' Before the light faded, and the land grew dark, they had walked in the garden belonging to the tavern, and then returned to the room, where they 'together and in company supped.'

They are Christopher Marlowe, and three men whom we have but glimpsed before—a conspectus, or hangman's summary, therefore, may be useful:

1. Ingram Frizer, servant to Thomas Walsingham.
2. Nicholas Skeres, his follower, who is to reappear in the records as working a fraud or two in concert with him.
3. Robert Poley, spy and complotter.

Although the scholars have been to some pains to show that at least two of these men were not Marlowe's social inferiors, the poet's last day on earth was talked away in the company of a deep and devious trio, viewed from any angle but the pedantic. And yet I do not believe that Marlowe was lured into an assassin's ambush. He was not the first poet to find delight in the society of rogues. One of

his companions was a man of parts and conversation—
Poley, who was able to brag, apparently truthfully, after
a battle of wits with the redoubtable Walsingham, that
'he putt Mr. Secretary into that heate that he looked out
of his wyndoe and grynned like a dogge.' As for the
others, they were, at the least, dabblers like himself in
affairs of state. Good talk he would have had there at
Widow Bull's; perhaps good food, certainly good cheer,
for they drank considerably. London was plague-ridden;
Marlowe nevertheless had to stay close at hand by order
of the Privy Council, and suburban Deptford, lying between Scadbury and the metropolis, was convenient from
every point of view. What the talk was about is not
known; it was not disclosed in the aftermath. Nor is there
any way of learning why the four men happened to come
together in Deptford, although it is not beyond conjecture. Thomas Walsingham may have sent his man Frizer
to inquire after Marlowe. Poley, who had returned that
day from The Hague, may have set out from Scadbury
with Frizer and Skeres.

This, then, is the setting—half in light, half in shadow.
Marlowe has been about ten hours in their company.
They have dined and strolled and supped, and are now
in their room. Marlowe, perhaps feeling the liquor he has
had, is stretched out on a bed. Frizer is at a table with his
back to Marlowe—or so he will shortly swear—and his
dagger hangs at his back, for comfort. At one end of the
table is Poley; at the other, Skeres. They are playing
backgammon.

There is a sudden scuffle; a thrust; and three men stand

huddled together. Perhaps Mistress Bull burst into the
room, saw the body, the poet's head streaked with clotted
red, and then, with a cry of horror, turned and rushed out.

A buzz rises from the street. In front of the tavern, a
cluster of excited Deptford citizens fills the air with an
ominous murmur.

2.

For more than twenty-four hours the body of Christopher Marlowe lay in the room of the tavern in Deptford.
Then came William Danby, Her Majesty's coroner, to
view it and impanel a jury for the inquest, for Deptford
was 'within the verge,' that is, within twelve miles of the
sovereign's person, and officers of her household had taken
charge of the proceedings. Frizer, Poley and Skeres,
meanwhile, were under arrest.

It is Friday, June 1. Coroner Danby calls his jurymen
together, explains what he has learned of the killing, cites
the law, and lets them view the body: 'Kent. / Inquisition
indented taken at Detford Strand in the aforesaid County
of Kent within the verge on the first day of June in the
year of the reign of Elizabeth by the grace of God of
England France & Ireland Queen defender of the faith
&c thirty-fifth, in the presence of William Danby, Gentleman, Coroner of the household of our said lady the
Queen, upon view of the body of Christopher Morley,
there lying dead & slain.'

The 'inquisition' does not tell us where the body was
viewed, or what position it was in—if in the tavern, as I

assume, whether on the bed or on the floor. Was the fatal dagger sheathed in Marlowe's head or in Frizer's scabbard? It names the jury—all worthy and law-abiding men—Nicholas Draper, Gentleman, Wolstan Randall, gentleman, William Curry, Adrian Walker, John Barber, Robert Baldwyn, Giles ffeld, George Halfepenny, Henry Awger, James Batt, Henry Bendyn, Thomas Batt senior, John Baldwyn, Alexander Burrage, Edmund Goodcheepe, & Henry Dabyns—and they give back to the coroner, and to posterity, the story they heard told, 'that when a certain Ingram ffrysar, late of London, Gentleman, and the aforesaid Christopher Morley and one Nicholas Skeres, late of London, Gentleman, and Robert Poley of London aforesaid, Gentleman, on the thirtieth day of May in the thirty-fifth year above named, at Detford Strand aforesaid in the County of Kent within the verge, about the tenth hour before noon of the same day, met together in a room in the house of a certain Eleanor Bull, widow; & there passed the time together & dined & after dinner were in quiet sort together there & walked in the garden belonging to the said house until the sixth hour after noon of the same day & then returned from the said garden to the room aforesaid & there together and in company supped; & after supper the said Ingram & Christopher Morley were in speech & uttered one to the other divers malicious words for the reason that they could not be at one nor agree about the payment of the sum of pence, that is, *le recknynge,* there; & the said Christopher Morley then lying upon a bed in the room where they supped, & moved with anger against the said Ingram ffrysar upon the words as aforesaid spoken between them, And the said Ingram then & there sitting in the room aforesaid with his back towards the bed where the said Christopher Morley was then lying, sitting near the bed, that is, *nere the bed,* & with the front part of his body towards the table & the aforesaid Nicholas Skeres & Robert Poley sitting on either side of the said Ingram in such a manner that the same Ingram ffrysar in no wise could take flight: it so befell that the said Christopher Morley on a sudden & of his malice towards the said Ingram aforethought, then & there maliciously drew the dagger of the said Ingram which was at his back, and with the same dagger the said Christopher Morley then & there maliciously gave the aforesaid Ingram two wounds on his head of the length of two inches & of the depth of a quarter of an inch; whereupon the said Ingram, in fear of being slain, & sitting in the manner aforesaid between the said Nicholas Skeres & Robert Poley so that he could not in any wise get away, in his own defence & for the saving of his life, then & there struggled with the said Christopher Morley to get back from him his dagger aforesaid; in which affray the same Ingram could not get away from the said Christopher Morley; and so it befell in that affray that the said Ingram, in defence of his life, with the dagger aforesaid of the value of 12*d.* gave the said Christopher then & there a mortal wound over his right eye of the depth of two inches & of the width of one inch; of which mortal wound the aforesaid Christopher Morley then & there instantly died.'

This, of course, is Frizer's account, corroborated by Poley and Skeres, whose lives were also in peril.

We are not told whether Eleanor Bull was questioned, or why Marlowe, Frizer, Skeres and Poley had met at her house. We do not know whether she or any other inmate of her house heard sounds of a quarrel on that fatal night, or whether, after the stabbing, aid was summoned, and by whom. The coroner's 'inquisition' tells us much, but leaves so much untold as to be baffling.

Was Frizer's dagger an ordinary flat blade? If so, the wound described would be almost impossible to inflict, save with determination born of intent. Was it a poniard, as some writers say, with a triangular or square blade? A blow with a poniard would account for the fatal wound.

There was a dispute over the bill. But there were two others present who had also eaten and drunk, and whose say in the matter was as great as either Marlowe's or Frizer's. It is not a point that seems to have occurred to Danby and his jury.

Frizer found it impossible, he said, to get away from Marlowe's sudden attack. But the table could have been pushed forward or overturned, or Poley and Skeres could have shoved the table aside, or rushed in, between the bed and the table, to separate the two men. What were they doing while the fight was in progress, for apparently it was not a matter of seconds? If this question was asked of them, the answer was not thought worth setting down.

The evidence of homicide in self-defense dwindles to Frizer's two scalp wounds and his uncontested story of the fatal assault. Commentators, studying Danby's document and cogitating the probabilities, have been skeptical. Not so his true sixteen: 'And so the Jurors aforesaid say upon their oath that the said Ingram killed & slew Christopher Morley aforesaid on the thirtieth day of May in the thirty-fifth year named above at Detford Strand aforesaid within the verge in the room aforesaid in the defence and saving of his own life, against the peace of our said lady the Queen, her now crown & dignity; And further the said Jurors say upon their oath that the said Ingram after the slaying aforesaid perpetrated & done by him in the manner & form aforesaid neither fled nor withdrew himself.' [1] But how long Frizer and his cronies waited before making the killing known, or whether the deed was first announced by another, does not appear.

The inquest over, Marlowe's body was borne off to the graveyard of St. Nicholas church, beside the royal docks of Deptford. What obsequies were said, or if they were left unsaid, and who followed the corpse of the poet to its final resting place, we do not know. But when earth had it, within the church, one of the religious, whom God had afflicted with deafness, wrote in the burial register:

Christopher Marlow slaine by ffrancis
ffrezer; the · 1 · of June.

3.

As the first step towards a royal pardon, Frizer immediately petitioned to bring his case into the Court of Chancery. On June 15 a writ of *certiorari* went to Coroner

Danby from the Queen: 'Elizabeth by the grace of God of England France & Ireland Queen Defender of the Faith &c To our well-beloved William Danby, Gentleman, Coroner of our household, greeting. Wishing for certain causes to be certified upon an indictment made in your presence concerning the death of Christopher Morley, upon view of the body of the same Christopher, at Detforde Strande in our County of Kent within the verge lying dead and slain, whence a certain Ingram ffrysar, late of London, Gentleman, is indicted (as by the record thence remaining with you it fully appears) And whether the same Ingram slew the aforesaid Christopher in self-defence, & not feloniously or of malice aforethought, so that in no other wise could he avoid his own death, or not; we command you to send the tenor of the indictment aforesaid with everything touching it and whatsoever names the parties aforesaid in that indictment are known by, to us in our Chancery under your seal distinctly & openly without delay, & with this your writ.' [2]

In reply, Danby submitted the inquisition made June 1, and Frizer was all but a free man, and with him his companions. Two weeks later Queen Elizabeth pardoned the slayer of her former servant. The pardon repeats Danby's inquisition almost word for word, and ends as follows: 'We therefore moved by piety have pardoned the same Ingram ffrisar the breach of our peace which pertains to us against the said Ingram for the death above mentioned & grant to him our firm peace Provided nevertheless that the right remain in our Court if anyone should wish to complain of him concerning the death above mentioned In testimony &c Witness the Queen at Kewe on the 28th day of June.'[3]

None, apparently, wished to complain, and the man in whose behalf her Privy Council had struck out six years before was forgotten. Not so some of his friends. On the following day, June 29, Justice Richard Young, one of Her Majesty's justices dealing with religious cases, had occasion to inform the Privy Council of a catch in the far-flung government net: 'yestar night, at ix of the cloke, Mr. Wilbrom came to me and brought Richard Chomley with him; he did submet hym selfe to hym.' And with the following sardonic remark Marlowe's 'disciple' slips beyond the margin of Justice Young's report and out of sight: 'Chomley sayd vnto my men as he was goyng to preson, that he did kno the Law, that when it came to pase, he cold shefte will ynowgh.'[4]

CHAPTER XXIV

Reckless Raleigh

I.

IT MIGHT be supposed, with Cholmley nabbed, and other recent happenings, that Sir Walter Raleigh, living in temporary retirement in the Norman castle the Queen had given him at Sherborne, Dorsetshire, would forego controversial talk touching religion—at least before those who could turn it to his harm. But it was not in the nature of the man to do so.

One day in the memorable summer of 1593, he and his half-brother Carew rode over to Wolverton to sup at the house of Sir George Trenchard. Prominent among the guests were Sir Ralph Horsey, Lord Lieutenant of the County, and the Reverend Ralph Ironside, minister of Winterbottom, who had brought with him a fellow minister and friend, the Reverend Mr. Whittle, vicar of Forthington. Supper went smoothly, until the wine Carew Raleigh had been imbibing loosened his tongue. What followed was reported to the Privy Council and then set down in writing by the Reverend Mr. Ironside for the perusal of a royal commission that came to investigate atheism and apostasy in Dorsetshire.

Deposed the divine: 'Towardes the end of supper some loose speeches of Mr. Carewe Rawleighes beinge gentlye reproved by Sir Raulfe Horsey in these wordes Colloquia prava corrumpunt bonés mores.[a] / Mr Rawleigh demaundes of me, what daunger he might incurr by such speeches? whervnto I aunswered, the wages of sinn is death. and he makinge leight of death as being common to all sinner & reightuous; I inferred further, that as that liffe which is the gifte of god through Jesus Christ, is life eternall: soe that death which is properlye the wages of sinne, is death eternall, both of the bodye, and of the soule alsoe.'

This nettled: 'Soule *quoth* Mr Carewe Rawleigh, what is that?'

Equally nettled, the divine replied: 'Better it were that we would be carefull howe the Soules might be saved, then to be curiouse in findinge out ther essence.'

At this point, Sir Walter entered the discussion, saying: 'I have benn a scholler some tyme in Oxeforde, I have aunswered vnder a Bachelor of Arte, & had taulke with diuines, yet heithervnto in this pointe (to witt what the reasonable soule of man is) have I not by anye benne resolved.'

After some urging, Mr. Ironside attempted a definition by way of Aristotle's *De Anima*, but Sir Walter objected that it was 'obscure, & intricate,' and the divine tried again: 'The reasonable soule is a sperituall & immortall substance breathed into man by god, wherby he lyves & moves & vnderstandeth, & soe is distinguished from other Creatures.'

---

[a] Evil communications corrupt good manners.

'Yea but what is that sperituall & immortall substance breathed into man &c. saieth Sir Walter.

'The soule *quoth* I.

'Naye then saieth he you aunswer not like a scholler.'

Before the reverend gentleman's pious generalities, Raleigh's contempt blazed forth. He had been drawn into the discussion, perhaps even against his inclination; certain it is, at least, that he did not begin it; but now that he had taken a stand, he would not draw back, Sir Ralph's presence notwithstanding. In the darkening room where faces glowed like lamps in the candle-light, his mind, skilled in logic and experience, began to glow like a jewel.

Pained at the aspersion on his scholarship, Mr. Ironside spluttered and writhed; in his own statement: 'I endevoured to prove that it was schollerlike, naye in such disputes as these, vsuall, & necessarye to runne in circulum; partlye because definicio rei was primum et immediatum principuum, and seinge primo non est prius, a man must of necessitie come backwarde & partelye becawse definicio & definitum be nature reciproce the one convertiblie aunsweringe vnto the question made vppon the other. As for example, if one aske what is a man? you will saye he is a creature reasonable & mortall; but if you aske againe. what is a creature reasonable & mortall, you must of force come backwarde, and aunswer, it is a man.'

The tree of his thought had shaken down a scatter of learned Latin scraps like leaden leaves, but now the tree stood naked to the wind of his opponent's wit: 'We have principles in our mathematickes sayeth Sir Walter, as totum est minus quamlibet sua parte. and aske me of it, and I can showe it in the table in the window in a man the whole beinge bigger then the partes of it.'

This is Ironside's recollection of what Raleigh said; we can only imagine the manner and the form in which he heard it—the marshalled words sent forth in glittering array to storm and take the minister's heights with axiom and art. Pressed hard now, Ironside fell back on his earlier manner, piously: 'I replied first that he showed quod est, not, quid est, that it was but not what it was; secondlye, that such demonstracion as that was against the nature of a mans soule being a sperite. for as his thinges beinge sensible were subiecte to the sence; soe mans soule being insensible was to be discerned by the sperite. nothinge more certaine in the worlde then that there is a god, yet beinge a sperite to subiecte him to the sence otherwise then perfected it is impossible.'

'Marrye *quoth* Sir Walter these 2 be like for neither coulde I lerne heitherto what god is.'

At this, a gentleman at the table of Sir George Trench- ard remarked 'that Aristotle shoulde saye he was Ens, Encium,' and the Rev. Mr. Ironside took it up: 'that god was ens entium a thinge of thinge havinge beinge of him selfe, & geivinge beinge to all creatures, it was most cer- taine, and confirmed by god him selfe vnto moyses.'

'Yea but what is this ens entium sayeth Sir Walter?'

'I aunswered it is God.'

Perhaps Raleigh now became aware of the expressions on the faces around him, for he requested that grace might be said by Mr. Ironside, 'for that *quoth* he is better then this disputacion.'

Thus went one summer evening in Elizabeth's England.

2.

Her Highness's Commission for Causes Ecclesiastical met at Cerne Abbas on March 21, 1594. Its two most important members were Thomas Viscount Howard of Bindon and Sir Ralph Horsey, Lord Lieutenant of the County of Dorsetshire, who had reproved Carew Raleigh at Sir George Trenchard's table, only to be regaled by Sir Walter. To guide them in their work the commissioners used nine 'Interro*gatories* to be ministred vnto such as ar to be exami*n*ed.' The ghost of Marlowe haunts the fourth: 'Item whome doe you knowe or have harde that hath spoken againste the truth of god his holye worde revealed to vs in the scriptures of the oulde & newe testament? or of some places therof? or have sayde those scriptures ar not to be believed & defended by her maiestie for doctrine, & faith, and salvacion, but onlye of policye, or Civell gouerment, and when & where was the same? And what other notice can you geive of anye such offender?' The others, and some of the answers to them, reveal that Raleigh and his friends had opened a provincial branch of the London 'school of atheism,' with a star pupil its ornament, one Lieutenant Thomas Allen of Portland Castle, a gallant with a grim and reckless humor— the fifth and sixth questions enshrine two of his *mots:* 'Item whome doe you knowe or have harde hath blasphemouslye cursed god: as in sayinge one time (as it rayned when he was a hawkinge) if there be a god A poxe on that god which sendeth such weather to marr our sporte? Item whome doe you knowe or have harde to have sayde, when he was dead his soule shoulde be hanged on the topp of a poale, and ronne god, ronne devill, and fetch it that woulde have it, or to like effecte?'

The answers to the 'interrogatories' leave no doubt as to the quarry:

John Jesopp, minister of Gillingham, sworn and examined, deposed that he 'hath harde that one Herryott of Sir Walter Rawleigh his howse hath brought the godhedd in question, and the whole course of the scriptures but of whome he soe harde it he doth not remember.'

William Hussey, churchwarden of Gillingham, 'hath harde Sir Walter Rawleigh susspected of Atheisme.'

John Davis, curate of Motcombe, 'hath harde Sir Walter Rawleigh by generall reporte hath had some reasoninge against the dietye of god, and his omnipotencye. And hath harde the like of Mr Carewe Rawleigh, but not soe directlye.'

Nicholas Jefferys, parson of Weeke Reges, went into some detail, he having a personal grievance: 'To the first Interogatory this deponent sayeth that he doth not knowe of his owne knowledge anye Atheistes within the Countie of Dorset or places neare adioyninge: but he hard by reporte of divers that Sir Walter Rawleigh and his retenewe ar generallye susspected of Atheisme; and especially one Allen of Portland Castle Leiftenant, And that he is a greate blasphemer & leight esteemer of Religion; and thereaboutes cometh not to Devine service or sermons.

'To the 3 he sayeth he hath harde that one Herriott attendant on Sir Walter Rawleigh hath ben convented before the Lordes of the counsell for denyinge the resur- reccion of the bodye.

'To the 6ᵗʰ Interogatory this deponent sayeth That aboute some three yeres paste cominge to Blandforde out of Hampsheire his horse was stayed & taken for a poste horse by Sir Walter Rawleigh & Mr Carewe Rawleigh; where this deponent entreatinge to have his horse released for that he was to ride home vnto his charge (from whence he had bene some tyme absent) to preach the nexte daye beinge sundaye, whervnto Mr Carewe Rawleigh replyed, that he this deponent might goe home where he woulde; but his horse shoulde preach before him.' [1]

Whether Raleigh himself or any of his retinue appeared before the examining commissioners is not known. Noth- ing seems to have resulted from the interrogatories except a lively text. There is no record of Harriot before the Privy Council, the parson of Weeke Reges notwithstand- ing.

But by devious ways, and in strange places, the whispers of atheism followed all whom Marlowe had known. Greene died repentant. Raleigh (while Elizabeth lived) and his follower Harriot somehow warded off evil. Cholmley was 'layd for' and imprisoned. Out of the once dazzling roster, one name remains. The fate of the man who bore it was the least spectacular; and yet, perhaps, he was most to be pitied.

CHAPTER XXV

The End of Kyd

I.

THE man for whom Marlowe had played—unwittingly, let us think—the role of evil angel was destined also to a tragic end.

It is not difficult to piece the remainder of Thomas Kyd's story together from the records that have escaped destruction. He dwells in them, the prisoner of his grief; his bruised spirit beats its wings against his words forever.

We have seen how he characterized his former roommate so that we seem to hear that distant, sardonic jester and blasphemer; we will now see a portrait of Kyd, by himself, etched in bitterness, and an addition, in hatred, to his picture of Marlowe.

It was not only that three sheets of an ancient theological dispute, copied out, had been found in his possession; from the imputation of heresy to the charge of atheism was but a step—and an informer took it. Between Kyd's arrest and Marlowe's death, someone lodged that fatal allegation with the authorities—perhaps the same Baines who had served Marlowe likewise. When that new stigma was once fastened on Kyd, he was a shunned man; the abhorrence with which he was thereafter regarded could not have been greater if he had come among men with the marks of the plague upon him.

The Lord Mayor's commissioners finally let him go. Emerging from prison, Kyd called on his master. He was received with caution. But he was apparently given to understand that if the authorities would send word that he was exonerated—that no further molestation was in store for him—he would be reinstated in his old post. Weak and emaciated after weeks of confinement and torture, the once proud, once successful author made his way to Westminster for an audience with Sir John Puckering, Lord Keeper of the Great Seal of England and now chief officer of Her Majesty's Privy Council. And he learned, as Dante had learned, as other after him have learned, 'How steep the stairs to great men's houses are.'

The interview turning out unsatisfactory, Kyd tried his luck with a letter; the pen stayed in his hand until all his heart's anguish was on paper: 'At my last being with your Lordship to entreate some speaches from you in my favor to my Lorde, whoe (though I thinke he rest not doubtfull of myne inocence) hath yet in his discreeter iudgment feared to offende in his reteyning me, without your honors former pryvitie; So is it nowe Right Honorable that the denyall of that favor (to my thought resonable) hath mov'de me to coniecture some suspicion, that Your Lordship holds me in, concerning Atheisme, a deadlie thing which I was undeserved chargd withall, & therfore have I thought it requisite, aswell in dutie to your Lordship, & the Lawes, as also in the feare of god, & freedom of my conscience, therein to satisfie the world and you.'

His hand shakes, his mind is on fire, as he marshals his arguments; then the shadow of Marlowe falls across his page: 'The first and most (thoughe insufficient surmize) that euer [? once] therein might be raisde of me, grewe thus. When I was first suspected for that Libell that concern'd the state, amongst those waste and idle papers (which I carde not for) & which vnaskt I did deliuer vp, were founde some fragments of a disputation, toching that opinion, affirmed by Marlowe to be his, and shufled with some of myne (vnknowne to me) by some occasion of our wrytinge in one chamber twoe yeares synce.'

He is careful not to say that the fragments of religious disputation are in Marlowe's handwriting, although if he could have shown that they were he could have saved himself much pain. He omits the matter of handwriting altogether, and I think it is significant that he does: for the professional script in which the pages are written are more likely to have been from his pen than from Marlowe's. Perhaps Marlowe had paid him, as a professional penman, to copy them out for him—another humiliation.

The shadow looms to ogre size: 'My first acquaintance with this Marlowe, rose vpon his bearing name to serve my Lord although his Lordship never knewe his service, but in writing for his plaiers, ffor never cold my Lord endure his name, or sight, when he had heard of his conditions, nor wold in deed the forme of devyne praiers vsed duelie in his Lordships house, haue quadred with such reprobates.

'That I shold loue or be familer frend, with one so irreligious, were verie rare, when *Tullie* saith *Digni sunt amicitia quibus in ipsis inest causa cur diligantur* [a] which neither was in him, for person, quallities, or honestie, besides he was intemperate & of a cruel hart, the verie contraries to which, my greatest enemies will saie by me.

'It is not to be nombred amongst the best conditions of men, to taxe or to opbraide the deade *Quia mortui non mordent*,[b] But thus muche haue I (with your Lordships favor) dared in the greatest cause, which is to cleere my self of being thought an *Atheist*, which some will sweare he was.

'ffor more assurance that I was not of that vile opinion, Lett it but please your Lordship to enquire of such as he conversd withall, that is (as I am geven to vnderstand) with *Harriot, Warner, Royden* and some stationers in Paules churchyard, whom I in no sort can accuse nor will excuse by reson of his companie, of whose consent if I had been, no question but I also shold haue been of their consort, for *ex minimo vestigio artifex agnoscit artificem.*' [c]

He was not of those usually found in Marlowe's company, but he names three members of Raleigh's group who were; although suddenly cautious, he parenthetically hedges his allegation—perhaps because he did not want Sir John to think he actually knew them; or there might be reprisals, and he has left himself a way out. Now he resumes: 'Of my religion & Life I haue alredie geven some instance to the Late comissioners & of my reverend

---

[a] Those are worthy of friendship in whom there resides a cause why they should be esteemed.

[b] Because the dead do not bite.

[c] The craftsman recognizes craft by the slightest trace.

meaning to the state, although perhaps my paines and vndeserved tortures felt by some, wold haue ingendred more impatience when Lesse by farr hath dryven so manye *imo extra caulas* [d] which it shall never do with me.

'But whatsoeuer I haue felt Right honorable this is my request not for reward but in regard of my trewe inocence that it wold please your Lordships so to [? mark] the same & me, as I maie still reteyne the favors of my Lord, whom I haue servd almost theis vj yeres nowe, in credit vntill nowe, & nowe am· vtterlie vndon without herein be somewhat donn for my recoverie. ffor I do knowe his Lordship holdes your honors & the state in that dewe reverence, as he wold no waie move the Leste suspicion of his Loves and cares both towards hir sacred Maiestie your Lordships and the Lawes wherof when tyme shall serve I shall geue greater instance which I haue observd.'

The word 'reward' in the foregoing paragraph strikes a jarring note. Had Kyd turned informer? Is that why, with bitterness welling up anew, he now hits back at the informer who lodged the charge of atheism against *him?* For this is how he concludes his epistle, quoting Cicero and St. Paul: 'As for the Libel Laide vnto my chardg I am resolued with receyving of ye sacrament to satisfie your Lordships & the World that I was neither agent nor consenting thervnto. Howebeit if some outcast *Ismael* for want or of his owne dispose to lewdnes, haue with pretext of duetie or religion, or to reduce himself to that he was not borne vnto by enie waie incensd your Lordships to suspect me, I shall besech in all humillitie & in the feare

---

[d] Even outside the fold.

of god that it will please your Lordships but to censure me as I shall prove my self, and to repute them as they ar in deed *Cum totius iniustitae nulla capitalior sit quam eorum, qui tum cum maxime fallunt id agunt vt viri boni esse videantur*[e] ffor doubtles even then your Lordships shalbe sure to breake [? into] their Lewde designes and see into the truthe, when but their Lyues that herein haue accused me shalbe examined & rypped vp effectually, soe maie I chaunce with *paul* to Liue & shake the vyper of my hand into the fier for which the ignorant suspect me guiltie of the former shipwrack. And thus (for nowe I feare me I growe teadious) assuring your good Lordship that if I knewe eny whom I cold iustlie accuse of that damnable offence to the awefull Maiestie of god or of that other mutinous sedition towrd the state I wold as willinglie reveale them as I wold request your Lordships better thoughtes of me that neuer haue offended you.'[1]

Something might be made of the image he chose from Paul—perhaps it sprang from subconscious knowledge of the pen that copied the disputation.

2.

If Kyd hoped to be recalled by Sir John Puckering for a pious account of his master's life, in which he would show to advantage, as being employed by him, he was disappointed. A request came instead for him to elaborate

[e] Since of all injustice none is more pernicious than that of those who, when they most deeply deceive, do it in such manner that they shall seem good men.

Marlowe's 'opinion' and the cautious reference to the late poet's intimates. He might have learned from this that his personal problem was not the concern of the great men in Her Majesty's government, but he complied eagerly—as regards the second item, once more cautiously: 'Pleaseth it your honorable Lordship toching marlowes monstruous opinions as I cannot but with an agreved conscience think on him or them so can I but particulariz fewe in the respect of them that kept him greater company. Howbeit in discharg of dutie both towardes god your Lordships & the world thus much haue I thought good breiflie to discover in all humbleness.

'ffirst it was his custom when I knewe him first & as I heare saie he contynewd it in table talk or otherwise to iest at the devine scriptures gybe at praiers, & stryve in argument to frustrate & confute what hath byn spoke or wrytt by prophets & such holie menn.

'1. He would report St John to be our savior Christes *Alexis* I cover it with reverence and trembling that is that Christ did loue him with an extraordinary loue.

'2. That for me to wryte a poem of St *paules* conversion as I was determined he said wold be as if I shold go wryte a book of fast & loose, esteeming *Paul* a Jugler.

'3. That the prodigall Childes portion was but fower nobles, he held his purse so neere the bottom in all pictures, and that it either was a iest or els fowr nobles then was thought a great patrimony not thinking it a parable.

'4. That things esteemed to be donn by devine power might haue aswell been don by observation of men all which he wold so sodenlie take slight occasion to slyp out

as I & many others in regard of his other rashnes in attempting soden pryvie iniuries to men did ouerslypp
thogh often reprehend him for it & for which god is my
witnes aswell by my lordes comaundment as in hatred of
his life & thoughts I left & did refraine his companie.'

We have seen this table talk before—it dates back two
years to the time Kyd and Marlowe shared chambers together. The reference to Marlowe's 'rashnes in attempting
soden pryvie iniuries to men' may be an echo of Frizer's
recent account of the sudden assault from behind in the
room in Deptford. But if Kyd really left Marlowe's company and stayed away, as he claimed, what are we to make
of his final accusation? 'He wold perswade with men of
quallitie to goe vnto the k[*ing*] of *Scotts* whether I heare
Royden is gon and where if he had liud he told me when
I sawe him last he meant to be.' [2]

It is apparent from this that Kyd had seen Marlowe recently—after his own release from prison and before the
killing at Deptford—and if he learned that Roydon had
gone to Scotland, it must have been from Marlowe that
he learned it. There is no signature to this second letter,
and it is possible that there was another sheet which has
disappeared. But their Lordships of the Privy Council
needed no further discrepancy to remark; although I do
not believe they were looking for discrepancies. Kyd had
served his turn; they had other matters to attend to; they
forgot about him.

A few scraps of paper, and man's perennially medieval
mind touching religion, had undone him.

3.

Plague closed the theaters. It seemed as though the hand of God and man were against him in his extremity. His chief talent was useless. He waited for word from Puckering or his master, rising with hope, going to bed forlorn, and waited in vain. The bitterness of the poor and scorned for the great and affluent was his; it poisoned his days. He was an outcast.

How he survived the bitter year of 1593 we do not know. Towards the end of the year he set himself the task of translating Garnier's *Cornelie*—original work was out of the question. Before the book appeared word of Kyd's plight reached the Countess of Sussex who, perhaps out of pity, proffered aid. Gratefully he dedicated the book to her in words that reveal his anguish: 'What grace that excellent Garnier hath lost by my defaulte, I shall beseech your Honour to repaire with the regarde of those so bitter times and priuie broken passions that I endured in the writing it. And so vouchsafing but the passing of a Winters weeke with desolate Cornelia, I will assure your Ladiship my next sommers better trauell with the tragedy of *Portia*. And euer spend one howre of the day in some kind seruice to your Honour, and another of the night in wishing you happiness.'

Winter, however, set in. His promise was never kept. He fades from men's sight under a stigma, and from official records officially cut off by his closest kin: 'Re-nunciation of the goods of Thomas Kyd. The thirtieth

day of the month of December in the year of Our Lord
1594, in the cathedral church of St. Paul, London, before
the venerable Thomas Creak, Doctor of Laws, Lord Arch-
deacon of London, officiating, etc., in the presence of me,
Sylvester Hulett, notary public, Deputy Register, etc.
There personally appeared Anna Kydd, wife of Francis
Kidd, father of the said Thomas Kidd, while he lived of
the parish of Saint Mary Colchurch, deceased, and in the
name of her said husband, as a related person, actually
exhibited an inventory of the said deceased person as true,
etc., and thus far, etc., and gave over the same into the
possession of the Register. And for divers causes and considerations (as she asserted) justly moving the mind of
her said husband in this sense, she wholly and expressly
renounced and refused in her husband's name (as above)
the burden of administration and title and interest of her
said husband in the goods, rights and credits of the said
deceased person, now or in the future.'[3]

What books, manuscripts and possessions soever the
author of *The Spanish Tragedie* might have gathered in
his career as a writer are dispersed among strangers, and
unlettered humanity sounds a thin, whining and disagreeable note, 'although the notary put an *etc*. in it,' as
Rabelais said. Did he die a martyr to the charge of atheism
—he who had boasted of his piety and the pious household in which he had served—perhaps by suicide, unable
to endure further privation and infamy?

CHAPTER XXVI

Shakespeare and Harvey

I.

'ART hath an enemy called Ignorance.'[1]
We have seen Gabriel Harvey thus far as a good,
if malicious reporter. He is about to reveal himself as
neither one nor the other, but merely misinformed.

It is a pity. With his nose for news, and his ear for gossip, much might have been added to our provocative
knowledge of Marlowe's last hours.

The summer of 1593 found Harvey once more in London, and indefatigably at work on a book entitled, somewhat exuberantly, *A New Letter of Notable Contents.
With a straunge Sonet, intitled Gorgon, or the wonderfull
yeare.* Three months after Marlowe's death it appeared.

It is the Epilogue to this book, dashed off, we can only
presume, at the last moment before press time, that concerns us. It contains the first published notice of the poet's
end. To write it, Harvey turned poet himself.

Unfortunately, he had no real notion of the nature of
poetry—his advice to Spenser shows that. This was the
view of the writers of his time, and his surviving verse
bears them out.

Harvey was not a frequenter of the suburbs. He has
heard, in London, that Marlowe is dead, and he must

needs put the news into his book. For reasons best known
to himself he chose to cast it in blank verse (with the first
line an imitation of his friend Spenser's 'Was it a dreame,
or did I see it playne'):

> Is it a Dreame? or is the *Highest minde*
> That euer haunted Powles or hunted winde,
> Bereaft of that same sky-surmounting breath,
> That breath that taught the Tempany to swell.

Hark now—his pen is poised for a colossal blunder:

> He & the *Plague* contended for the game:
> The hawty man extolles his hideous thoughtes,
> And gloriously insultes upon poore soules,
> That plague themselves: *for faint harts plague
> themselves.*

So here it is, in part; a poor thing, but his very own; a
poem about the tragedy at Deptford; but there is no
tavern here, no conspirators, no quarrel and no dagger-
man—plague was the antagonist, and plague, says Harvey,
won:

> The graund Dissease disdain'd his toade Conceit,
> And smiling at his tamberlaine contempt,
> Sternely struck-home the peremptory stroke,
> He that not feared God, nor dreaded Diu'll,
> Nor ought admired but his wondrous selfe.

Could anything be more foolish than these vain lines ringing with timid admiration for the dead dramatist? What did Harvey think of them when he learned the truth? What inspiration might have been his had he only taken the trouble to verify the circumstances of Marlowe's death personally, as he had done the year before when Greene lay dying.

The news of Marlowe's death reached St. Paul's and the taverns frequented by the writers he had known a little more accurately. How some of them felt may be seen in George Peele's spontaneous apostrophe, immediately inserted in his new poem, *The Honour of the Garter*:

> Unhappy in thy end,
> *Marley*, the Muses' darling.

2.

Shakespeare's reaction was similar.

About this time, or very shortly after, he was at work on Act Three of a new play to be called *As You Like It*. And ever and anon as he worked the image of Marlowe and of the tavern room wherein he was struck down flashed into his mind, attended by memories of their association, of the dead man's great achievements and of a promise that was as great. 'To judge of Poets is only the facultie of Poets; and not of all Poets, but the best.' [2] He could judge; and on this occasion he judged with regret, perhaps with grief. Then he put it into words, which was relief of a sort for the present; later he returned to the theme (*vide* Sonnet 86),[3] for he never quite forgot the youth from Canterbury.

The allusions to Marlowe in *As You Like It* sound topical. They serve no useful dramatic purpose; they enlarge no one's character, and do not further the action of the play. But there they are, sprinkled throughout Act Three, and taken together they tell something of Shakespeare's feelings after hearing about the deed at Deptford. This is the first one, preparatory and tentative, but significantly enough, Ovid reappears at life's end as at the beginning of Marlowe's career:

> Touchstone. I am here with thee and thy goats, as the most capricious poet, honest Ovid, was among the Goths.
> Jaques. (aside) O knowledge ill-inhabited, worse than Jove in a thatch'd house!

There is nothing in this exchange to prepare one for the astonishing *riposte* that follows from the mouth of Touchstone: 'When a man's verses cannot be understood, nor a man's good wit seconded with the forward child understanding, it strikes a man more dead than a great reckoning in a little room.'

Is not this Deptford in epitome? The reference to Mistress Bull's tavern reckoning, ostensible cause of the fatal quarrel, is clear enough; is there also to be found here a defense of Marlowe's table talk, which offended only when not rightly understood? Of the echo from a famous line in *The Jew of Malta* it is perhaps not necessary to say anything.

Shakespeare returns to the theme, this time via Celia: 'the oath of a lover is no stronger than the word of a tapster; they are both the confirmers of false reckonings.'

And he takes his leave of Marlowe in this play with a tender saluation in homage to the poet who wrote *The passionate Sheepheard to his loue* and the greater homage of a borrowed line (from *Hero and Leander*):

> Dead shepherd, now I find thy saw of might:
> 'Who ever lov'd that lov'd not at first sight?' [4]

CHAPTER XXVII

Memories of Marlowe

I.

TO SCADBURY in 1597 came Queen Elizabeth, and was sumptuously entertained by Thomas Walsingham and his lady. As a result, plain Tom became Sir Thomas, and his wife was made a lady of Her Majesty's bedchamber. Soon after, two dedications attested to their new-gained honors—one to each, and both concerned Marlowe. For in the following year there appeared two editions of *Hero and Leander*.

The first was important on two accounts: it gave to the world Marlowe's bright fragment, and contained a tribute to his memory, from one Renaissance gentleman to another, which offsets considerably the accounts of him given by his enemies.

The second was also remarkable; it offered, in Chapman's continuation of the poem, a startling apostrophe to Marlowe's spirit which has bewildered the scholars and delighted all lovers of 'the Muses' darling.'

The first, published by Edward Blount, was dedicated by him to Marlowe's old friend and patron, now 'the Right Worshipfull, Sir Thomas Walsingham, Knight': '*Sir, wee thinke not our selues discharged of the dutie wee owe to our friend, when wee haue brought the breathlesse bodie to the earth: for albeit the eye there taketh his euer farwell of that beloued obiect, yet the impression of the man, that hath beene deare vnto vs, liuing an after life in our memory, there putteth vs in mind of farther obsequies due vnto the deceased. And namely of the performance of whatsoeuer we may iudge shal make to his liuing credit, and to the effecting of his determination preuented by the stroke of death.'* [1]

The incense of pleasant hours in Marlowe's company rises from these lines; and there is at least a hint that Blount and Walsingham saw the poet buried.

This, and the following dedication to Walsingham's wife, go far to neutralize a sensational thesis that the poet was assassinated at the instigation of Lady Audrey. It would have been scandalous—even in that cynical era—to accept the honor of a dedication under the circumstances.

2.

Now comes George Chapman, to add the candle of his genius to the great light that still brightened the air. A double opportunity lures him: honor to the dead, and— God willing—credit for the living; but if ever a lumbering wagon was hitched to a star, his continuation of *Hero and Leander* is it. Except, of course, for the apostrophe to Marlowe.

Now Chapman took the business of being an author with great seriousness. Merely putting pen to paper, and paper through press, was not enough. He must go

HERO
AND
LEANDER.

By Christopher Marloe.

LONDON,
Printed by Adam Islip,
for Edward Blunt.
1598.

wreathed in bays, and Jove's lightning must dart about his head—or, at the least, in the background. Therefore, in his writings, as in his portraits, one finds a considerable amount of mysterious matter. Thus, in his Dedication of the completed *Hero and Leander,* he records a 'strange instigation' that drew him to this work, as earlier he had acknowledged the aid of 'that most assistful and unspeakable Spirit' while translating the *Iliads:* 'TO MY BEST ESTEEMED AND WORTHELY HONORED LADY, THE LADY WALSINGHAM, one of the Ladies of Her Maiesties Bedchamber. *I present your Ladiship with the last affections of the first two Louers that euer* Muse *shrinde in the Temple of* Memorie; *being drawne by strange instigation to employ some of my serious time in so trifeling a subiect, which yet made the first Author, diuine* Musaeus, *eternall.*'

And so forth. It is written in Chapman's typical vein, affected and fawning: '*This poore Dedication (in figure of the other vnitie betwixt Sir* Thomas *and your selfe) hath reioynd you with him, my honoured best friend, whose continuance of ancient kindnes to my still-obscured estate, though it cannot encrease my loue to him, which hath euer been entirely circulare; yet shall it encourage my deserts to their vtmost requitall, and make my hartie gratitude speake; to which the vnhapines of my life hath hetherto been vncomfortable and painful dumbnes.*' [2] But of Marlowe there is not a word.

Yet the man had fire in him; and as soon as his continuation of *Hero and Leander* was well under way, it blazed forth, as though the 'instigation' to which he has referred really meant something. For in the very midst of

his labors he is suddenly made aware of Marlowe's spirit
in the sky:

> Then thou most strangely-intellectual fire,
> That proper to my soule hast power t'inspire
> Her burning faculties, and with the wings
> Of thy vnspheared flame visitst the springs
> Of spirits immortall; Now (as swift as Time
> Doth follow Motion) finde th' eternall Clime
> Of his free soule, whose liuing subiect stood
> Vp to the chin in the Pyerean flood,
> And drunke to me halfe this Musean storie,
> Inscribing it to deathles Memorie:
> Confer with it, and make my pledge as deepe,
> That neithers draught be consecrate to sleepe.
> Tell it how much his late desires I tender,
> (If yet it know not) and to light surrender
> My soules darke offspring, willing it should die
> To loues, to passions, and societie.

Not all of it is understandable (it would not be Chapman's if it were); but what is clear will serve, and serving it may provide the clue with which to unravel the mystery of Shakespeare's sonnet *86*, the sonnet of the 'rival poet,' where the images projected by Chapman in his apostrophe to Marlowe are apparently repeated.

3.

The sonnet contains, besides the astonishing climax of the rival poet sequence (78-86), references to two varie-

ties of nocturnal phenomena: viz, a ghost, and some spirits
—the former specific, the latter, general. These spirits,
and that ghost, offer the best clues Shakespeare has left us
with which to identify his rival, but the scholars appear to
have assumed that the ghost, which appears in the sestet,
is merely a continuation of the spirit imagery in the octave.
Yet spirits are one thing, and a ghost is another, as Shakespeare, it safely may be assumed, knew.

Sonnet 86: The Octave
Was it the proud full sail of his great verse
Bound for the prize of all too precious you,
That did my ripe thoughts in my brain inhearse,
Making their tomb the womb wherein they grew?
Was it his spirit, by spirits taught to write
Above a mortal pitch, that struck me dead?
No, neither he, nor his compeers by night
Giving him aid, my verse astonished.

Herein is depicted a poet who is also an invoker of
spirits. Nebulous identifications of him have been attempted; indeed, a legion of Elizabethan poets, great and
obscure, has been summoned up as Shakespeare's rival.
The most plausible hypothesis makes him George Chapman. But while *Sonnet 86*, the sparkling gem of the rival-
poet cluster, can be made to fit the famous translator of
Homer, the scholars ingeniously involved their task by
considering the fourteen lines as a unit, as has been in-
dicated, when, as will be seen, an important change in
diction and imagery takes place between the octave and

sestet—indeed, it makes its appearance in the seventh and eighth lines of the octave; for none but scholars would ever believe that a 'compeer by night' is the same as a spirit rising out of the dark.

Sonnet 86: The Sestet
He, nor that affable familiar ghost
Which nightly gulls him with intelligence,
As victors of my silence cannot boast;
I was not sick from any fear of thence.
But when your countenance fill'd up his line,
Then lack'd I matter; that enfeebled mine.

So specific is this new characterization, it seems only reasonable to assume that Shakespeare had someone in mind besides the invoker of spirits. The words 'affable' and 'familiar,' as well as 'ghost,' as distinct from the 'spirits' of the octave, are too carefully chosen, too carefully placed, to be only a continuation of the earlier images. They appear, rather, to be an additional stroke, as if by their means Shakespeare was making identification of his rival complete to his coterie, if not to all his contemporaries. (Although not published until 1609, at least some of Shakespeare's verses were circulating as early as 1598, when they were referred to as 'sugred *Sonnets* among his priuate friends'.) Literary spirits are mere poetic formulae; but 'affable familiar ghost' is a human tribute, an echo of past friendship. The new words point to one recently deceased, who had stood in a definite relationship to the author of the sonnet and the rival poet.

These considerations lead back, inevitably, to Chapman's apostrophe to Marlowe's spirit. If Chapman is indeed the rival poet of the *Sonnets*, the role of 'affable familiar ghost' must be assigned to the dead author of *Hero and Leander*.

4.

The scholars have taken Chapman's apostrophe to mean that Marlowe asked him to finish his poem. This is a puerile notion. Why any poet in his prime should ask another to finish a work of his simply passes understanding. We know now that Marlowe, stabbed in the head, did not have time for literary bequests, or any bequests whatsoever. 'His late desires' can only mean that, before the affair at Deptford, he had been at work on the Musaean theme of Hero and Leander; 'if yet it knows not' shows clearly that Marlowe did not know before his death that Chapman would continue where he left off. But what follows—'And drunke to me halfe this Musean storie'—may mean that Marlowe had once told Chapman about the work under way, or had read the unfinished manuscript to him. Only this, and nothing more.

Now this was Chapman's way; in 1598, for his own purposes, Marlowe

stood
Vp to the chin in the Pyerean flood,

and he communed with the dead poet's spirit; but in 1616, he published his own version of *The Divine Poem of Musaeus, first of all bookes, translated according to the originall.* There, in the epistle 'to the commune reader,' something crabbed that dwelt in his soul issued forth: 'When you see *Leander* and *Hero,* the subjects of this Pamphlet, I persuade myself your prejudice will increase to the contempt of it; either headlong pre-supposing it all one, or at no part matchable with that partly excellent Poem of Maister Marloe's. For your all one, the Works are in nothing alike; a different character being held through both the style, matter, and invention. For the match of it, let but your eyes be matches, and it will in many parts overmatch it.'

He happened to be mistaken.

5.

The ghost of *Sonnet 86,* the spirit of Chapman's apostrophe, reappear in the dedication of *Lucans* FIRST BOOKE, translated by Marlowe at Cambridge, and published in London in 1600. Thomas Thorpe, who nine years later was to bring out Shakespeare's *Sonnets,* thus inscribed *Lucan* to Edward Blount, publisher of *Hero and Leander:* 'Blount: *I purpose to be blunt with you, & out of my dulnesse to encounter you with a* Dedication *in the memory of that pure Elementall wit* Chr. Marlow; *whose ghoast or* Genius *is to be seene walke the* Churchyard *in (at the least) three or foure sheets. Me thinks you should presently looke wilde now, and growe humorously frantique vpon the tast of it. Well, least you should, let mee tell you. This spirit was sometime a familiar of your own,* Lucans first booke translated; *which (in regard of your old right in it) I haue rais'd in the circle of your Patronage.'* [3]

Marlowe's line-for-line version of Lucan's *Pharsalia* belongs as we have seen to his earliest period of authorship. Blount may have found the poem among the papers left by Marlowe at Scadbury, but appears to have transferred his right in it to Thorpe. Thorpe's reference to St. Paul's churchyard, where the book went on sale at 'the Signe of the Flower de Luce,' is followed by a pun on the sheets of the quarto.

These are the slim facts and slight conjectures to be extracted from the prose of Thomas Thorpe. Nevertheless, we get from him, as earlier from Blount, an *'impression of the man, that hath beene deare vnto vs, liuing an after life in our memory'*—of *'that pure Elementall wit* Chr. Marlow.'

CHAPTER XXVIII

The Army of the Lord

I.

THE Puritan tide of obloquy rose slowly, but it finally overwhelmed the memory of Marlowe. Their story of a divine visitation on the man and his works carried all before it. Within a century of his death even writers attempting a critical estimate of his achievements were under the spell of his calumniators. The wrath finally spent itself, but the righteousness stayed. Those who had known him and might have defended him were dead; his books had all but disappeared.

The outburst of Puritan wrath against Marlowe is without parallel in literature. No vile epithet was too vile for his detractors to use, yet most of them wrote only from hearsay, or merely embroidered one another's accounts, hardly one able to contain his gloating—religious caterpillars of the new style, who

> prove their doctrine orthodox
> By apostolic blows and knocks,

as the first Samuel Butler wrote.

In the tragic end of the poet who blazed the trail that Shakespeare followed they saw only the terrible justice of heaven appropriately meted out, and added fuel to the fiery legend which has persisted to this day of Marlowe as the very archetype of Elizabethan roaring boy—hot-blooded, bellicose, wearing pride like a feather in his hat, and iniquitous before God and man. In truth, he sat for this portrait, distorted though it is; but there was something else, as we have seen.

Four years after Marlowe's death, Thomas Beard called the roll of the sinners, foreign and domestic, Marlowe among them, in his *Theatre of Gods Iudgements*. He characterized the poet thus: 'Not inferiour to any of the former in Atheisme & impiety, and equall to all in manner of punishment was one of our own nation, of fresh and late memory, called *Marlin*, by profession a scholler, brought vp from his youth in the Vniuersitie of Cambridge, but by practise a playmaker, and a Poet of scurrilitie, who by giuing too large a swinge to his owne wit, and suffering his lust to haue the full raines, fell (not without iust desert) to that outrage and extremitie, that hee denied God and his sonne Christ, and not only in word blasphemed the trinitie, but also (as it is credibly reported) wrote bookes against it, affirming our Sauiour to be but a deceiuer, and *Moses* to be but a coniurer and seducer of the people, and the holy Bible to be but vaine and idle stories, and all religion but a deuice of pollicie. But see what a hooke the Lord put in the nosthrils of this barking dogge: It so fell out, that in London streets as he purposed to stab one whome hee ought a grudge vnto with his dagger, the other party perceiuing so auoided the stroke, that withall catching hold of his wrest, he stabbed

his owne dagger into his owne head, in such sort, that notwithstanding all the meanes of surgerie that could be
wrought, hee shortly after died thereof. The manner of
his death being so terrible (for hee euen cursed and
blasphemed to his last gaspe, and togither with his breath
an oth flew out of his mouth) that it was not only a mani-
fest signe of Gods iudgement, but also an horrible and
fearefull terrour to all that beheld him. But herein did
the iustice of God most notably appeare, in that hee com-
pelled his owne hand which had written those blasphemies
to be the instrument to punish him, and that in his braine,
which had deuised the same.'

A year later, Francis Meres, cataloguing the authors of
his time in *Palladis Tamia*, wrote: 'As *Iodelle*, a French
tragicall poet beeing an Epicure, and an Atheist, made a
pitifull end: so our tragicall poet *Marlow* for his Epicur-
isme and Atheisme had a tragicall death; you may read
of this *Marlow* more at large in the *Theatre of Gods iudg-
ments*, in the 25. chapter entreating of Epicures and
Atheists.'

But not content with referring his readers back to
Beard, Meres gave his own version of the affair: 'As the
poet *Lycophron* was shot to death by a certain riual of his:
so *Christopher Marlow* was stabd to death by a bawdy
Seruing man, a riuall of his in his lewde loue.'

2.

In 1600, William Vaughan, though aping Beard's style,
published an independent version of Marlowe's death in

The Golden Grove and, as will be seen, he hits the mark several times: 'Not inferiour to these was one Christopher Marlow by profession a play-maker, who, as it is reported, about 7. yeeres a-goe wrote a booke against the Trinitie: but see the effects of Gods iustice; it so hapned, that at Detford, a litle village about three miles distant from London, as he meant to stab with his ponyard one named Ingram, that had inuited him thither to a feast, and was then playing at tables, he quickely perceyving it, auoyded the thrust, that withall drawing out his dagger for his defence, hee stabd this Marlow into the eye, in such sort, that his braines comming out at the daggers point, hee shortlie after dyed. Thus did God, the true executioner of diuine iustice, worke the ende of impious Atheists.'

What Ingram's surname was, and what the quarrel, did not concern Vaughan, who seized on the moral and pointed it out. Nor, apparently, did he trouble himself with the fact that there had been two earthly witnesses, besides God's angels. 'Tables' is backgammon.

Beard's version was again given, somewhat abridged, but still titillating to the pious, in 1618 by Edmund Rudierde in a work entitled *The Thunderbolt of Gods Wrath against Hard-Hearted and stiffe-necked sinners:* 'We read of one *Marlin*, a *Cambridge* Scholler, who was a Poet, and a filthy Play-maker, this wretch accounted that meeke seruant of God *Moses* to be but a Coniurer, and our sweete Sauiour but a seducer and a deceiuer of the people. But harken yee braine-sicke and prophane Poets, and Players, that bewitch idle eares with foolish vanities: what fell vpon this prophane wretch, hauing a quarrell against one whom he met in a streete in London, and would haue stabd him: But the partie perceiuing his villany preuented him with catching his hand, and turning his owne dagger into his braines, and so blaspheming and cursing, he yeelded vp his stinking breath: marke this yee Players, that liue by making fooles laugh at sinne and wickednesse.'

It is a good example of the style and sentiments of the soldiers in that army of the Lord that eventually conquered England and shut the theaters.

Ten years after Rudierde, John Earle, in his *Microcosmographie*, concluded his portrait of a 'pot-poet' as follows: 'Sitting in a Baudy-house, hee writes Gods Iudgements. Hee ends at last in some obscure painted Cloth, to which himselfe made the Verses, and his life like a Canne too full spils vpon the bench. He leaues twenty shillings on the score, which my Hostesse looses.'

This also hits the mark. 'Painted Cloth' means wall hangings or tapestries.

Some fifty years later, so vague had the legend of Marlowe's death become, that John Aubrey, of the delectable *Brief Lives*, makes Ben Jonson the slayer: 'He killed Mr. Marlow, the poet, on Bunhill, comeing from the Green Curtain play-house.' Aubrey's double-dealing friend, Anthony à Wood, drew on both Beard and Meres, especially the latter, recognizing that the love interest heightens the drama and that the triangle is deadly. Thus Wood on Marlowe in *Athenae Oxonienses*, 1691: 'But see the end of this person, which was noted by all, especially by the Precisians. For it so fell out, that he being

deeply in love with a certain Woman, had for his rival a
bawdy serving man, one rather fit to be a Pimp, than an
ingenious *Amoretto* as *Marlo* conceived himself to be.
Whereupon *Marlo* taking it to be a high affront, rush'd
in upon, to stab, him, with his dagger. But the serving
man being very quick, so avoided the stroke, that with
all catching hold of *Marlo's* wrist, he stab'd his own dagger into his own head, in such sort, that notwithstanding
all the means of surgery that could be wrought, he shortly
after died of his wound.'

The reader is also in great danger of a stroke, with
'rush'd in upon, to stab, him,' etc. 'Precisians' are our
friends the Puritans.[1]

Such, then, are their accounts of the man who, in his
life and work, adventured in new realms of the spirit, and
who wrote for all to mark:

> I count Religion but a childish Toy,
> And hold there is no sinne but Ignorance.

CHAPTER XXIX

A Backward Glance

I.

THE Queen who had honored the Walsinghams was dead; a new monarch reigned; but the light of the Elizabethan age continued to glow.

Forty-two years after Kyd and Marlowe sojourned together, to part enemies, Thomas Heywood, who had known both in his youth, brought *The Jew of Malta* back to the stage, and then saw it through the press. His edition, dated 1633, is not the authoritative text a first edition would be, but it possesses at least one distinctive attribute: a Prologue praising Marlowe and Edward Alleyn, creator of the title roles in Marlowe's dramas.

Heywood wrote the Prologue to usher in the old play on the stage of the Cockpit Theatre; and considering that he himself has confessed to having had a hand or 'at least a main finger' in 220 plays, which means that he knew and collaborated with most of the dramatists of his time, beginning in the reign of Elizabeth, his praise of Marlowe is all that it should be:

We know not how our Play may passe this Stage,
But by the best of* Poets in that age   **Marlo.*
The Malta Jew had being, and was made;
And He, then by the best of* Actors play'd.   **Allin*

The Famous

TRAGEDY
OF
THE RICH IEVV
OF *MALTA.*

AS IT WAS PLAYD
BEFORE THE KING AND
QVEENE, IN HIS MAJESTIES
Theatre at *White-Hall,* by her Majesties
Servants at the *Cock-pit.*

Written by CHRISTOPHER MARLO.

LONDON;
Printed by *I. B.* for *Nicholas Vavasour,* and are to be sold
at his Shop in the Inner-Temple, neere the
Church. 1633.

2.

It may be that the new production of Marlowe's old play quickened the aging writer's nostalgia into sharp recollection, for in his *Hierarchie of the blessed Angells*, which appeared two years later, Heywood takes a fond backward glance at the bright era of his youth, invoking its great figures by name. The passage is a *dramatis personae* for this book:

> *Greene,* who had in both Academies ta'ne
> Degree of Master, yet could neuer gaine
> To be call'd more than *Robin:* who had he
> Profest ought saue the *Muse,* Serv'd, and been Free
> After a seuen yeares Prenticeship; might haue
> (With credit too) gone *Robert* to his graue.
> *Marlo,* renown'd for his rare art and wit,
> Could ne're attaine beyond the name of *Kit;*
> Although his *Hero* and *Leander* did
> Merit addition rather. Famous *Kid*
> Was call'd but *Tom. Tom. Watson,* though he wrote
> Able to make *Apollo's* selfe to dote
> Vpon his Muse; for all that he could striue,
> Yet neuer could to his full name arriue.
> *Tom. Nash* (in his time of no small esteeme)
> Could not a second syllable redeeme.

Chapman is there by implication, *via* the addition to *Hero and Leander;* of Shakespeare he wrote:

Mellifluous Shake-speare, whose inchanting Quill
Commanded Mirth or Passions, was but *Will*.

And, finally, of himself:

I hold he loues me best that calls me *Tom*.

And so we leave them, Robin and Kit, four Toms and
one Will, all passion spent, all quarrels past.

Notes

Notes

CH. I. 1. *Fragmenta Regalia,* 1641; reprinted by Arbor, 1870. 2. Conyers Read, *Mr. Secretary Walsingham,* 1925. 3. Dasent, *Acts of the Privy Council,* XV, p. 141. Mr. Leslie Hotson was the first to call attention to it in his now famous book, *The Death of Christopher Marlowe,* 1925. Newly transcribed by Bakeless, *The Tragicall History of Christopher Marlowe,* 1942, p. 77. I have portrayed Walsingham going over the minutes, as it is extremely unlikely that any business of the Council would have escaped him.

CH. II. 1. Somerset Maugham's *Of Human Bondage* describes King's School in modern times; his hero also found it irksome. Maugham returns to the theme in *The Summing Up:* 'I grew older. I went to the King's School. The masters were clergymen; they were stupid and irascible.'

CH. III. 1. Strype, *Life of Parker,* 1831, III, p. 386 f. 2. This most agreeable discovery, together with Mistress Benchkin's will, was made by Mr. Frank W. Tyler of Canterbury, who placed the documents at the disposal of Mr. Bakeless, who used them, *op. cit.,* I, viii and 74 *et seq.* John Marlowe's deposition is in the Public Record Office, Canterbury, 39/11. 3. Perhaps Marlowe showed Thomas Nashe his *Dido;* it is at least possible that only someone who knew of the play as a Cambridge composition could have called attention to it after Marlowe's death, when it was first published. Nashe's name actually got on the title-page of the 1594 edition; but the only thing to connect Nashe with this play, the evidence of versification and imagery being all in favor of Marlowe, is a supposed elegy on Marlowe's death, written by Nashe, which was inserted in some copies of the book, apparently after the book was off the press. Two eighteenth century scholars, Tanner and Warton, writing independently of each other, say they saw a copy of *Dido* with Nashe's elegy, but neither one had the wit to copy the poem. It is now one with 'what song the Sirens sang.' 4. Homer appears to have prefigured both Virgil and Marlowe: 'Pitiless that thou art, the knight Peleus was not then thy father, nor Thetis thy mother, but the grey sea bare thee, and the sheer cliffs, so untoward is thy spirit' (Iliad, Book XV). 5. Greg, *Henslowe's Diary*, II, p. 12.

CH. IV. 1. Milton has two poems about Hobson, 'On the University Carrier,' and 'Another of the Same.' No. 509 of *The Spectator* gives an account of the man and his trade. 2. Dekker, *The Seuen deadlie Sinns of London*, 1606 (Oxford, 1922). Stow, *Suruey of London*, *passim*. 3. Elizabethan slang: *doxies*, mistresses to rogues; *priggers of prancers*, horse-stealers; *kinching coes*, young male rogues; *dummerers*, beggars pretending dumbness; *jarkmen*, clerkly rogues; *dells*, female beggars, still maidens; *bawdy baskets*, female pedlars; *queans*, harlots. 4. Greg, *op cit*.

CH. V. 1. Wood, *Athenae Oxonienses*.

CH. VI. 1. Plutarch's Antony hails his sons by Cleopatra as rulers over Armenia, Media, Parthia; Phoenicia, Syria and Cilicia. 2. The problem of Marlowe's apocryphal plays which bear a relation to Shakespeare—such as the source-plays of *Henry VI*—will be taken up in a subsequent work. 3. It is to a famous scene in the Second Part that the most famous allusion of all was made, by Shakespeare—good-naturedly, I believe. The idea for Marlowe's hero drawn by captive kings came from *Jocasta*, to which reference has been made. Marlowe's scene was easy to burlesque; and when Pistol (in *Henry IV*) does so it probably was good for a laugh with the spectators. The humor appears to have gone out of it. 4. Malory has a forecast of Drake's fireships: 'So it befell on a time that the miscreant Saracens landed in the country of Cornwall soon after these Sessoins were gone. And then the good Prince Boudwin, at the landing, he raised the country privily and hastily. And or it were day he let put wild-fire in three of his own ships, and suddenly he pulled up the sail, and with the wind he made those ships to be driven among the navy of the Saracens. And to make short tale, those three ships set on fire all the ships, that none were saved' (*Morte D'Arthur*, Book X, Ch. XXXII). 5. *The Prayer-Book of Queen Elizabeth*, in the Ancient and Modern Library of Theological Literature, 1890, Appendix XII, p. 225. 6. Homer again: 'But if I might somewhere find Aias of the loud war-cry, then both together would we go and be mindful of battle even were it against the power of heaven' (*Iliad*, Book XVII).

CH. VII. 1. A chapter heading in Rabelais reads: 'A propheticall riddle in the style of Merlin.' The fool in *King Lear* remarks: 'This prophecy Merlin shall make; for I live before his time.' Greene's pun is clearer when it is remembered that 'Merlin' was pronounced 'Marlin.' 2. McKerrow's *Nashe*, III, p. 85.

CH. VIII 1. The earliest English version of the German *Historia von D. Johann Fausten*, 1587, that has come down is dated 1592; but the title-page shows there was an edition before it by the phrase 'Newly imprinted.' For a discussion of dates and a transcription of 'source passages,' see Boas, *The Tragical History of Doctor Faustus*, 1932.

CH. IX. 1. For the information contained in this chapter and Ch. X, I am indebted to Mark Eccles' brilliant book, *Christopher Marlowe in London*, 1934. I have done little more than arrange the documents in sequence. Bradley's petition against Swift, Alleyn and Watson is in the Public Record Office,

London, K.B. 29/226, membrane 119, and was originally discovered by Mr. Hotson, who turned his find over to Mr. Eccles.

CH. X. 1. Middlesex Sessions Roll 284, no. 12. 2. Chancery Miscellanea, bundle 68, file 12, no. 362. 3. Middlesex Sessions Roll 284, no. 1. 4. Patent Rolls 32 Eliz., part 4. All four documents are in Eccles, *op. cit.* The coroner's inquest and Queen's grace documents were translated from the Latin for the present work.

CH. XI. 1. John Aubrey tells it thus: 'He loved a wench well; and one time getting up one of the Mayds of Honour against a tree in a Wood ('twas his first lady), who seemed at first boarding to be something fearfull of her Honour, and modest, she cryed, Sweet Sir Walter, what doe you me ask? Will you undoe me? Nay, sweet Sir Walter! Sweet Sir Walter! Sir Walter! At last, as the danger and the pleasure at the same time grew higher, she cryed in the extacey, Swisser Swatter! Swisser Swatter! She proved with child.' (*Brief Lives*, Oxford, 1898). 2. The surrender of Smerwick, in Ireland, was followed by the slaughter of the entire garrison of 600; Raleigh was one of the officers in charge of the wholesale executions. 3. Naunton, *op. cit.* 4. I am indebted to my friend, Mr. Willard R. Trask, for calling Reinoso's poem to my attention, and it is his English rendering which I have used. 5. *The Compleat Angler.* 6. Stevens, *Thomas Hariot and his Associates*, 1900. 7. See Ch. XXII. 8. Excerpted from an English summary of Parsons' *Responsio ad Elizabethae Edictum*, concerning the edict of 1591 against the Catholics. 9. *Pierce Penilesse.*

CH. XII. 1. The title of this chapter is, of course, Ben Jonson's phrase in his poem to Shakespeare, but towards the end of his life his judgment took another turn: 'The true Artificer will not run away from nature, as hee were afraid of her; or depart from life, and the likenesse of Truth; but speake to the capacity of his hearers. And though his language differ from the vulgar somewhat; it shall not fly from all humanity with the *Tamerlanes*, and *Tamer-Chams*, of the late Age, which had nothing in them but the *scenicall* strutting, and furious vociferation, to warrant them then to the ignorant gapers.' (*Timber: or, Discoveries*, 1641). 2. Dekker, *op. cit.* 3. Englished by Ezra Pound. 4. With this, Marlowe's play ends. He was not one to moralize, and the moralizing chorus which enters at this point was probably the product of other hands, paid four pounds by Henslowe for 'ther adicyones in doctor fostes' (Greg. *op. cit.*, I, p. 172). Goethe's praise of Marlowe's masterpiece—'How greatly is it all planned'—is a classical example of appreciation expiating a crib; compare his opening with Marlowe's:

> *Faust.* Alas! I have explored
> Philosophy, and Law, and Medicine;
> And over deep Divinity have pored, etc. (Anster's trans.)

CH. XIII. 1. The evidence for such an assumption is skilfully set forth by Dr. S. A. Tannenbaum, *The Booke of Sir Thomas More*, 1927. 2. See Ch. XXV and Notes. 3. See Brooke, *Works*, 1910; Bennett, *The Jew of Malta*, 1931, and Bakeless, *op. cit.*, for discussion of sources.

CH. XIV. 1. Middlesex Sessions Roll 309, no. 13. Discovered by Eccles; *op. cit.*, p. 105.

CH. XV. 1. Englished by Eccles, *op. cit.*, p. 166.

CH. XVI. 1. D. B. Wyndham Lewis, *Francois Villon*, 1928. 2. The passage is strikingly reminiscent of Socrates' utterance in the *Phaedo*: 'Will you not allow that I have as much of the spirit of prophecy in me as the swans? For they, when they perceive that they must die, having sung all their life long, then sing more beautifully than ever. . . .'

CH. XVIII. 1. Although *Edward II* has come down to us, in the Quarto of 1594, with few textual flaws, there is at least one scene wherein lines are obviously missing and must be conjectured to arrive at Marlowe's meaning. An attempt is made here (conjectured lines in *italics*):

> *Lan.* Monster of men,
> That like the Greekish strumpet traind to armes
> And bloudie warres, so many valiant knights
> *Leadest to doom,*
> Looke for no other fortune wretch then death,
> Kind *Edward* is not heere to buckler thee.
>   *War.* Lancaster, why talkst thou to the slaue?
> Go souldiers take him hence, for by my sword,
> His head shall off: *Gaueston*, short warning
> Shall serue thy turne: it is our countries cause,
> That here seuerelie we will execute
> *The look'd-for penalty of ciuill broiles*
> Vpon thy person: hang him at a bough.
>   *Gau.* My Lord.
>   *War.* Souldiers, haue him away:
> But for thou wert the fauorit of a King,
> Thou shalt haue so much honor at our hands
> *As to be 'headed.*
>   *Gau.* I thanke you all my lords, then I perceiue,
> That heading is one, and hanging is the other,
> And death is all.

(ll. 1182-1199, Brooke's ed.)

CH. XIX. 1. Sir Simonds D'Ewes, *A Complete Journal of the Votes, Speeches and Debates both of the House of Lords and House of Commons throughout the whole Reign of Queen Elizabeth of Glorious Memory*, 1693, p. 505 *et seq.* For an account of the cloth trade fostered by the aliens, and its importance in the nation's history, see Trevelyan, *A Shortened History of England*, 1942, pp. 190-193. 2. See Tannenbaum's account, *op. cit.*, regarding the conjectured authorship of this work. 3. *The Book of Sir Thomas More*, Malone Society Reprint, 1911, sig. A. See also Brooke, *The Shakespeare Apocrypha*, 1918, pp. xlvii-liv. 4. Dasent, *op. cit.*, Vol. XXIV, p. 222.

CH. XX. 1. Harleian MS. 6848, fol. 187-189. 2. Dasent, *op. cit.*, Vol. XXIV, p. 244.

CH. XXI. 1. Dryden, in *Religio Laici:*

> Are there not many points, some needfull sure
> To saving Faith, that Scripture leaves obscure?
> Which every Sect will wrest a several way
> (For what *one* Sect interprets, *all* Sects *may:*)
> We hold, and say we prove from Scripture plain,
> That *Christ* is God; the bold *Socinian*
> From the *same* Scripture urges he's but MAN.
> Now what Appeal can end th' important suit;
> *Both* parts *talk* loudly, but the *Rule* is *mute.*

2. Dasent, *op. cit.*, Vol. XXIV, p. 244.

CH. XXII. 1. The 'Note,' calculated to make Marlowe smart, has managed, latterly, to startle and abash finicky scholars who have come upon it—not without a secret blush or two; for they have either suppressed it or strewn it with asterisks after tasting its heady comminations. 2. Harleian MS. 6848, fol. 185-86. 3. Harleian MS. 6853, fol. 307-308. 4. Harleian MS. 6848, fol. 190-191. 5. Tannenbaum, *The Assassination of Christopher Marlowe*, 1928, implicates Raleigh. 6. Naunton, *op. cit.* 7. Whitsun Eve, 1593, fell on June 2, whereas Marlowe was killed May 30. 'Within iii dayes' gets the date right, and I can only assume, with others, that the word 'after' is a subconscious blunder of the scribe.

CH. XXIII. 1. Chancery Misc., bundle 64, file 8, no. 241; original in Latin. 2. *Ibid.* 3. Patent Rolls, 1401; original in Latin. The documents concerning Marlowe's death and his slayer's pardon were discovered and transcribed by Mr. Hotson, *op. cit.* 4. Harleian MS. 7002, fol. 10.

CH. XXIV. 1. The disputation, and the questions and depositions of witnesses are from Harleian MS. 6849, fol. 183-190. A complete transcription is given in G. B. Harrison's *Willobie his Avisa*, Bodley Head Quartos, 1926, Appendix III, pp. 255-271.

CH. XXV. 1. Harleian MS. 6849, fol. 218. The handwriting of this letter is the ordinary secretary script for the English portions and Roman scrivener's for the Latin. The latter resembles the handwriting of the 'vile hereticall Conceiptes' found in Kyd's chamber; but this is not necessarily significant—the style is a formalized one, and other hands of the period resemble it. 2. Harleian MS. 6848, fol. 154. 3. *The Archdeaconry of London Probate and Administration Act Book* (Boas, *The Works of Thomas Kyd*, 1901).

CH. XXVI. 1. Jonson, *Every Man Out of His Humor.* 2. *Timber: or, Discoveries.* 3. See Ch. XXVII, Section III. 4. The quotation from *Hero and Leander* would indicate that the edition of this poem licenced in September, 1593, actually appeared, although no copy has come down to us (see Brooke, *Works*, p. 485). Shakespeare, however, may have seen the poem in manuscript.

CH. XXVII. 1. Brooke, *op. cit.*, p. 491. 2. *Ibid.*, pp. 513-514. 3. *Ibid.*, p. 647.

CH. XXVIII. 1. By the eighteenth century the wrath had been squeezed dry, and the accent was on lewdness: 'This Author was both a Poet and a Player; but in the Opinion of some Contemporary Writers, a Man of bad Morals. Having an intrigue with a loose woman he came unexpectedly into her Chamber, and caught her in the Embraces of another Gallant. This so much enraged him that he drew his Dagger, and attempted to Stab him; but, in the Struggle, the Paramour seized Marlow, turned the Point into his Head, and killed him on the spot' (*Theatrical Records*). In the nineteenth, the story became: 'In May (1593) we know that Marlowe was at the little village of Deptford, not many miles from London. There was turbulent blood there, and wine; there were courtesans and daggers. Here Marlowe was slain, killed by a serving-man, a rival in a quarrel over bought kisses' (Havelock Ellis in the *Mermaid Marlowe*). A Victorian circumlocution. In the twentieth century, there appeared the following stricture, in an article entitled *Marlowe and the Heavy Wrath of God:* 'The evils of Marlowe's chief characters were also Marlowe's own, and he, like these characters, fell to be plagued in hell' (F. Paul in *American Catholic Quarterly Review*).

Selected Bibliography

The Works of Christopher Marlowe, edited by C. F. Tucker Brooke, Oxford, The Clarendon Press, 1910.

The Works and Life of Christopher Marlowe, general editor, R. H. Case, London, Methuen, New York, Lincoln MacVeigh, The Dial Press: *The Life of Marlowe* and *Dido, Queen of Carthage,* C. F. Tucker Brooke, 1930; *Tamburlaine,* U. M. Ellis-Fermor, 1930; *The Jew of Malta* and *The Massacre at Paris,* H. S. Bennett, 1931; *Poems,* L. C. Martin, 1931; *Doctor Faustus,* F. S. Boas, 1932; *Edward II,* H. B. Charlton and R. D. Waller, 1933.

The Death of Christopher Marlowe, by Leslie Hotson, London, Nonesuch Press, 1925.

Christopher Marlowe in London, by Mark Eccles, Cambridge, Mass., Harvard University Press, 1934.

Christopher Marlowe, A Biographical and Critical Study, by F. S. Boas, Oxford, The Clarendon Press, 1940.

The Tragicall History of Christopher Marlowe, by John Bakeless, Cambridge, Mass., Harvard University Press, 1942.

Index

267